UKRAINIAN
SECURITY
POLICY

THE WASHINGTON PAPERS

. . . intended to meet the need for an authoritative, yet prompt, public appraisal of the major developments in world affairs.

President, CSIS: David M. Abshire

Series Editor: Walter Laqueur

Director of Studies: Erik R. Peterson

Director of Publications: Nancy B. Eddy

Managing Editor: Donna R. Spitler

MANUSCRIPT SUBMISSION

The Washington Papers and Praeger Publishers welcome inquiries concerning manuscript submissions. Please include with your inquiry a curriculum vitae, synopsis, table of contents, and estimated manuscript length. Manuscript length must fall between 120 and 200 double-spaced typed pages. All submissions will be peer reviewed. Submissions to *The Washington Papers* should be sent to *The Washington Papers*; The Center for Strategic and International Studies; 1800 K Street NW; Suite 400; Washington, DC 20006. Book proposals should be sent to Praeger Publishers; 90 Post Road West; P.O. Box 5007; Westport, CT 06881-5007.

The Washington Papers/167

UKRAINIAN SECURITY POLICY

Taras Kuzio

Foreword by
Nicholas S. H. Krawciw

**PUBLISHED WITH
THE CENTER FOR STRATEGIC
AND INTERNATIONAL STUDIES
WASHINGTON, D.C.**

PRAEGER

Westport, Connecticut
London

Library of Congress Cataloging-in-Publication Data

Kuzio, Taras.
    Ukrainian security policy / Taras Kuzio.
        p. cm. – (The Washington papers ; 167)
    "Published with the Center for Strategic and International Studies
Washington, D.C."
    Includes index.
    ISBN 0-275-95384-X (hard cover). – ISBN 0-275-95385-8 (soft
cover)
    1. National security–Ukraine. 2. Ukraine–Foreign
relations–1991– 3. Ukraine–Military policy. I. Title.
II. Series.
DK508.849.K89 1995
327.47'71'009049–dc20   95-19071

British Library Cataloging in Publication data is available.

Library of Congress Catalog Card Number: 95-19071
ISBN: 0-275-95384-X (cloth)
        0-275-95385-8 (paper)

First published in 1995

Praeger Publishers, 88 Post Road West, Westport, CT 06881
An imprint of Greenwood Publishing Group, Inc.

Printed in the United States of America

∞™

The paper used in this book complies with the Permanent
Paper Standard issued by the National Information Standards
Organization (Z39.48-1984).

10 9 8 7 6 5 4 3 2 1

Contents

Foreword

Since 1991, when today's Ukraine declared its independence from the disintegrating Soviet Union, very few scholars of international security trends have had the background and perseverance to monitor that country's developing and, at times, puzzling security policy. The most notable among them has been and is Taras Kuzio. When not in his native England, he spends frequent and extended periods of time in Kiev or in other parts of Ukraine observing, listening, and learning all about this new state's (and ancient nation's) political, sociological, and security trends. His research has focused on Ukraine's political and historical legacy, its emerging defense issues, its developing processes for security policy formulation, and the role of its dominant personalities in Ukrainian security affairs.

In this work, Taras Kuzio depicts the emerging geopolitical significance of Ukraine with all its concomitant political internal and external ramifications. His insights and his account are a historic record of the rebirth of Ukraine's defense and security structure and of the debates shaping its security policy. Moreover, his analysis clearly portrays the dilemma faced by many new nations: how to build national awareness, new institutions, and broad consensus while simultaneously providing security and stability in an economically weak and politically polarized country.

From this volume, Western policymakers and scholars will gain a better understanding of Ukraine's distrust of Russia and the West, its hesitancy to give up nuclear weapons in 1992–1993, and its desire to be part of Europe. Kuzio makes it clear that most Ukrainian leaders understand Russia's strategy to preserve its influence and political leverage over Ukraine and their need to deflect Russian pressures while continuing to consolidate their country's independence and ties with the West. He also details Ukrainian concerns about territorial integrity and other threat perceptions. Kuzio's presentation of the many social and sociological challenges facing Ukraine as it reduces, reorganizes, and rebuilds its still too large armed forces is truly complete in its scope and insight.

Today, Ukraine's security policy continues to emphasize the rebuilding and development of primarily conventional defense forces. Linked with this goal is Ukraine's determination to salvage as much of its military-industrial base as possible, including most of its space industry. Progress in all aspects of the Ukrainian defense program is hindered by lack of funds, by a corroding industrial infrastructure, and by generally low morale among service personnel (particularly draftees) and the workforce. Meaningful organizational or functional reforms are visible only here and there. Conventional modernization needed to address a wider range of threats is being delayed pending economic improvement.

Despite this seemingly downward spiraling trend, the spring and summer of 1995 brought some signs of success. With strong U.S. and European political and financial backing, President Kuchma's administration took steps toward market reform that portend a possible turnaround of Ukraine's fortunes. The national security arena witnessed Ukraine's steady progress in denuclearization, with its accompanying flow of some compensation and good will from the West for that compliance, and in "Partnership for Peace" activities with NATO and particularly with the United States. The economy has a chance for improvement, and the task of addressing military reductions as well as modernization may gain some momentum. To be sure, many pitfalls remain. Problems involving potential internal instability, Russian pressures, and the situations in Crimea and along the borders with Moldova, as well as the Black Sea Fleet dispute, are far from resolved.

Taras Kuzio's *Ukrainian Security Policy* lays out a complete panorama of factors involved in these and many other issues. It is an invaluable reference for understanding the complexities, dangers, and opportunities Ukraine still faces. As such, it is a most comprehensive source of mutually beneficial policy options for Ukraine, its neighbors, and the West.

Major General Nicholas S. H. Krawciw, USA (Ret.)

About the Author

Taras Kuzio is research fellow at the Center for Russian and East European Studies, University of Birmingham, England, and an honorary research fellow at the School of Slavonic and East European Studies, University of London. He is editor of *Ukraine Business Review* and joint editor of *East European Monitor*, as well as the Ukraine-Moldova editor of *Jane's Sentinel*. Mr. Kuzio has served as research associate at the International Institute for Strategic Studies and has written extensively on former Soviet nationality problems and contemporary Ukrainian affairs. He is joint author of *Ukraine: Perestroika to Independence* (1994), as well as the author of two shorter studies under prophetic titles, *Ukraine: The Unfinished Revolution* (1992) and *Russia-Crimea-Ukraine: Triangle of Conflict* (1994).

Note on Transliteration

The transliteration of place names in this study are from Ukrainian, not Russian, as was common during the existence of the Soviet Union. The new transliterations are taken from "Russia and the Newly Independent Nations of the Former Soviet Union," map supplement to *National Geographic* magazine, March 1993. The only exception is the city of Kiev, which is well known in this transliteration (in Ukrainian, Kyyiv). The transliteration of notes is by the modified Library of Congress transliteration system.

Summary

In December 1991, Ukrainian voters overwhelmingly endorsed independence in a referendum leading to the USSR's disintegration and the end of the cold war. Ukraine at once faced a host of domestic and foreign problems. Its first priority was to create security forces to address perceived external threats—mainly from Russia, whose leaders have found it difficult, if not impossible, to accept Ukrainian independence. And during 1992 and 1993, relations between Ukraine and the West were clouded by Ukraine's ambivalent nuclear weapons policies, as well as by a largely Russocentric and one-dimensional U.S. foreign policy.

This volume reviews the major elements and sources of Ukrainian security policy. An overview chapter sets the study in historical context, reviewing the legacy of regional divisions and territorial threats to Ukrainian independence, such as the Crimea. The next chapter outlines the main domestic challenges to Ukrainian independence. The chapters that follow discuss Ukrainian foreign and military policies, including nuclear weapons, the Black Sea Fleet, and Russian policies toward Ukraine.

Ukraine's twin legacies of external domination and Soviet totalitarianism have left a profound mark on the Ukrainian ruling elites and population. The impact of this history and the perceived threats to territorial integrity have led Ukraine to prioritize state- and security-building measures. Ukraine inherited a historical legacy of regional divisions, conflicting foreign orientations and potential border disputes that have prevented its forming a public consensus on national interests and security policy. For the sake of its territorial integrity, Ukraine must maintain an orientation that is neither nationalistic nor pro-Russian.

The new Ukrainian leadership elected in 1994 has understood that the chief short-term threats to Ukrainian independence are domestic—the economic and energy crises, uneven levels of national consciousness, and growing separatism. If these threats continue to escalate, the role of the security forces will increase, as will the danger of authoritarianism.

In the medium to long terms, Russian assertiveness and intervention in the Commonwealth of Independent States could increase external threats to Ukraine. The stability of Ukraine depends on the normalization of relations with Russia as well as political and financial support from the West.

Introduction

Of the former Soviet republics, the most important to European security are undoubtedly the Russian Federation and Ukraine. Ukraine is larger than France, exceeds 52 million in population, and possesses abundant natural resources—all of which make it a strategically important new European state. Its many ethnic minorities include 11 million Russians (whose welfare directly concerns Russia), and on its territory it has inherited large armed forces, military equipment, and nuclear weapons.

Ukraine is important to European security in several respects. It borders four central European countries—Poland, Slovakia, Hungary, and Romania—all of which have national minorities in Ukraine. It also borders Moldova, the home of a large Ukrainian minority and the scene of armed conflict between the Moldovan authorities and Russian-backed separatists. Hungary and Poland regard an independent Ukraine as vital to their national interests and as a buffer between themselves and Russia; if Ukraine were reincorporated within a Russian empire, their feelings of insecurity would rise.

All four central European countries have an interest in Ukraine's stability. A prolonged economic crisis, civil war, or Russian-Ukrainian conflict leading to massive regional social unrest would bring large numbers of refugees, many of them national minorities, into central Europe. Civil war or a conflict with Russia could spill over into central Europe, and damage to any of

1

Ukraine's large number of nuclear power stations could precipitate an environmental crisis.

Any or all of these factors would require central European countries to spend a larger amount of their gross national products on their ministries of Defense and Interior, to relocate troops and border guards to their eastern borders, and to institute a visa system for residents of the former USSR. Their programs of economic reform would be disrupted, especially in the case of Hungary and Poland.

Ukraine is also crucial to European security because of its deep-seated conflict with Russia. Instability arising from socioeconomic and ethnic factors would produce a vacuum into which Russia might be tempted to venture, thereby creating regional instability and large numbers of refugees. The disintegration of Ukraine could also lead to the growth of separatism within Russia, especially in the adjacent northern Caucasus and among the already restless Tatars. Armed conflict in the Crimea would inflame relations between Moscow, the north Caucasus, and the Tatar autonomous republic within the Russian Federation.

A Russian-Ukrainian conflict would be disastrous for central and eastern Europe on a far greater scale than the civil war in former Yugoslavia. If Ukraine were reintegrated within Russia, either partially—by incorporating large areas with Russian minorities—or completely, it would recreate a large empire resembling the former USSR, which could lead to another cold war with the West. It would also deflect Russian attention away from domestic political and economic reform by concentrating upon empire building. An independent, democratic, and prosperous Ukraine is therefore central to promoting Russia's transformation into a postimperial power.

At the same time, Ukraine's reluctance until recently to abide by its numerous commitments to denuclearize contributed to destabilization in central-eastern Europe, worsened relations with Russia (which is highly unlikely to accept a nuclear Ukraine), increased its isolation from the West, and severely damaged the Nuclear Nonproliferation Treaty. Nuclear weapons will not improve Ukrainian security. Their continued possession for emotional, historical, economic, psychological (not military) reasons is merely a substitute for elaborating a comprehensive Ukrainian security policy as well as national interests that would define real threats, specify how to deal with them, and identify those with broad national consensus.

This volume examines the domestic sources that shape and influence Ukraine's security policy as well the foreign and defense policies undertaken by the Ukrainian leadership. It analyzes Ukraine's evolution from a highly stable country with great economic potential in early 1992 to a source of instability in central-eastern Europe. Which mistakes were made by the Ukrainian leadership? What role did external pressure and foreign disinterest play in Ukraine's growing instability? Why were Ukraine's leaders reluctant to implement reform? Indeed, what is the likely outcome of domestic developments in Ukraine and Russia? How will growing regionalism in Ukraine affect Ukrainian-Russian relations?

Chapter 1 of this volume presents the historical context of Ukrainian security policy and outlines its relevance for contemporary policy-making—which requires an understanding of the forces that shape Ukrainian security policy. In particular, it discusses Ukraine's historical legacy of lengthy external domination, its failure at previous attempts to obtain independence, its weak and uneven levels of national consciousness, and the effects of territorial changes and contemporary conflicts. As in all postcommunist countries, Ukrainian security policy is being formulated from scratch, at times creating confusion, misconceptions, and mistakes along the way. Ukraine, unlike Russia, failed to inherit the large and professional diplomatic and journalistic cadres of the former Soviet Union.

Chapter 2 analyzes the domestic sources of Ukrainian security policy, focusing on the role of key groups in formulating security policy and threats. This chapter examines the role of policymakers—president, parliament, and political party and civil-military leaders—in formulating Ukrainian foreign and defense policies. What influence do they each have? Who wields greatest influence? What role do different levels of power (president, parliament, and government) play in formulating Ukrainian policies? How do the competing domestic and regional constituencies influence the decision-making process? Why did Ukraine adopt economic and monetary policies that have proved to be so disastrous?

This volume also identifies the large number of real and perceived threats to Ukrainian independence that confront Ukrainian foreign and defense policies. External territorial claims against Ukraine, although they do exist, are unlikely in the short to medium term to become military threats to Ukrainian security. The only exception is the Crimea, one of Europe's greatest potential flash points. It possesses an entire range of factors that could lead to local conflict and then involve both Ukraine and Russia. Russian leaders are unanimously unable to accept Ukrainian sovereignty over the Crimea. Ukrainians perceive Russian demands for naval basing rights in Sevastopol and the election of a pro-Russian separatist president as the beginning of a process that could lead to its eventual loss of the entire Crimean peninsula.

In addition, regionalism elsewhere in the Donbas and Transcarpathia parallel the growing domestic political and economic crisis. Further aggravation of relations with Russia could transform these demands into separatism. Good relations with Russia and a benevolent Ukrainian leadership sensitive to national minority demands are therefore essential to maintain Ukraine's territorial integrity.

To a great extent, external threats are exaggerated. They are based on a deep sense of insecurity that pervades the Ukrainian political elite, clouding its understanding of the outside world and making it highly suspicious (Ukraine's "Pereiaslav complex") of the motives of other countries—particularly Russia. Ukrainian insecurity is also driven by the fear that a large proportion of the population and officer corps within the armed forces would be disloyal in the event of a conflict with Russia. Ukrainian foreign and military policies thus focus on the search for security and protection of territorial integrity.

Still, this volume does highlight the dangers of Russian-Ukrainian conflict in the near future. Russia has dropped reform and nation building in favor of establishing a new empire within the former USSR. The Russian domestic political agenda has moved perceptibly to the right. The differences between democrats and nationalists with regard to security policies toward the "Near Abroad" have narrowed to such an extent that it only amounts to a question of the policies used to implement the same final goal. These factors, coupled at the dawning of the Yeltsin era, will bring new challenges, frustrations, and dangers in Russian-Ukrainian relations.

Chapter 3 examines the military policies of Ukraine's leaders. Although Ukraine inherited a large array of military equipment from the former USSR, its military bases and units are located away from Ukraine's primary external security threat – Russia. Ukraine and Russia continue to dispute the division and ownership of these assets, especially the Black Sea Fleet and nuclear weapons.

Ukraine has largely succeeded in nationalizing former Soviet armed forces and equipment on its territory, both preventing the establishment of foreign military bases and ensuring that nearly three-quarters of a million former Soviet troops pose no potential threat to the newly independent state. Russian military bases are thus not available to support separatist movements or coup plotters as they are in the Transcaucasus and central Asia – except for Sevastopol, where Russian naval basing rights could stimulate separatist and pro-Russian tendencies throughout the Crimea.

At the same time, the large numbers of armed forces inherited from the former USSR, together with the many Ukrainian officers outside the republic within the former USSR, a great proportion of whom may decide to return to Ukraine, will create a socioeconomic burden for the government and will be difficult to integrate into Ukrainian society. If Russian-Ukrainian relations continue to deteriorate and the Ukrainian domestic crisis deepens further, the influence of the armed and security forces within Ukraine will grow. The armed forces are too closely tied to the *raison d'etre* of the newly independent state and its territorial integrity.

Ukraine has de facto nationalized the strategic nuclear weapons on its territory. It is likely to denuclearize completely only in the medium to long term and already controls all aspects of these weapons on its territory (although Ukraine still lacks operational control). During 1992–1993, this volume argues, Ukrainian nuclear policy was ambiguous, given the lack of a coherent security policy. During this period the West's Russia-first policy consigned the geopolitical space of the former USSR to Russia. The only exceptions were the three Baltic republics. Ukraine remained an ambigious case for the West. Without nuclear weapons, the West may have also consigned Ukraine to Russia's geopolitical sphere of influence. In other words, without nuclear weapons, Ukraine would have been treated like Moldova—not Estonia—by the West.

Nevertheless, Ukrainian insecurity and unstable developments in neighboring Russia are likely to drag out the process of denuclearization. If a nationalist president and government takes power in post-Yeltsin Russia, full Ukrainian denuclearization is unlikely.

The final chapter identifies emerging trends and directions in Ukrainian security policy. Will an independent Ukraine survive the domestic crisis and external pressures and threats it faces? Will it be sucked back into the Russian sphere of influence, like Belarus and Georgia, or learn to maintain a balance between the foreign orientations of its different regions? Is a Ukrainian-Russian conflict likely to occur (especially over the Crimea)? How will President Leonid Kuchma's policies affect Ukraine's geostrategic orientation?

This volume concludes by outlining policy recommendations for Ukraine's relations with the West, Russia, and central Europe. It suggests ways the West can address Ukrainian insecurity, isolation, and reliance upon nuclear weapons and work to integrate Ukraine into a new European security architecture.

1

Ukraine's Political Legacies

In December 1991, newly independent Ukraine inherited profound legacies of external domination and totalitarian rule. In the thirteenth century, Ukrainian territories had been divided among different external powers. Only after World War II were they reunited within the former USSR. As a result, Ukraine's nation-building process was never completed.

These regions often had conflicting approaches to the outside world, neighboring countries, political and economic reform, and Soviet and Ukrainian historical myths and symbols. Because earlier drives to achieve independence had failed, Ukraine now placed high priority on building its armed forces, developing social and ethnic stability, and integrating the former *ancien* regime to widen the base of support for the newly independent state. The price for this alliance between some nationalists and communists has been high, particularly on the reform process. Previous failures to achieve independence also produced broad consensus on the need to build an independent state and ensure its security, even at the expense of other requirements.[1]

Since the summer of 1994, Ukrainian policy under President Leonid Kuchma has increased the priority given to nation-building and domestic problems, especially the economic crisis and corruption. The June 1994 presidential elections in Ukraine confirmed the historical legacy of a divided nation and polity. Both candidates in the final round obtained nearly a 50:50 split in the vote along regional lines, reflecting the two conflicting orientations of the population (Western and Eurasian).

The Legacy of External Domination

Ukrainian territories were only reunited after World War II, following seven centuries of separate development after the medieval state of Kiev Rus' disintegrated in the thirteenth century. Since then, western and eastern Ukraine have been mainly under Polish-Austrian and Russian rule respectively, which has given them different regional characteristics, political and social outlooks, and attitudes toward the outside world.

All three East Slavic nations—Russia, Ukraine, and Belarus—trace their origins to Kiev Rus', the state that from the eighth to the thirteenth centuries covered most of the territory of the former European USSR. The thirteenth-century invasion of the Mongol Tatars placed the three east Slavic nations under different rulers. The majority of Ukrainian territories eventually became a part of the Polish-Lithuanian commonwealth.

The Polish-Russian contest over Ukrainian territories dominated the sixteenth through eighteenth centuries, a period punctuated by Ukrainian Cossack revolts against the Poles and Russians with Tatar and Swedish aid. Although the 1654 Treaty of Pereiaslav between Ukraine and Russia guaranteed Ukrainian "autonomy," this was gradually reduced by the end of the eighteenth century when the bulk of Ukrainian territories were incorporated within the Tsarist Russian empire.

Although Russian and Soviet historiography praise the Treaty of Pereiaslav as the "reunion" of Russia and Ukraine, Ukrainian political and literary elites as well as preeminent historians have traditionally regarded it as a national disaster.[2] They have compared the unfavorable fate of Ukrainians under the Tsarist empire to the plight of western Ukrainians under more liberal Austrian rule. As a consequence of external domination, Ukraine's ruling elite was assimilated by the eighteenth century.

This legacy of extended external domination and separate development of Ukrainian territories has produced a major division between the western and eastern regions. The western Ukrainian region's 10 million population, 5.4 million of whom live in Galicia, plays a role disproportionate to its small size within the republic. By the onset of World War I, Galician Ukrainians living in the Austrian-Hungarian empire had enjoyed more than 150 years of education, from elementary to higher levels, in their mother tongue. The Ukrainian Catholic (Uniate) Church was legalized, and Ukrainian newspapers and cooperative and cultural societies flourished. Ukrainians also participated in Austrian politics after 1848 with their own political parties, while charitable, sports, women's, and mutual assistance organizations evolved. During World War I, Ukrainians formed their own separate armed units within the Austrian-Hungarian army.[3]

In contrast to the relatively liberal plight of western Ukrainians under Austrian and Polish rule, eastern Ukrainians were subjected to Russification. Until 1905, eastern Ukrainians had no publications of their own, and the Ukrainian language was banned by two separate edicts in 1863 and 1876. The Ukrainian Autocephalous Orthodox Church was absorbed into the Russian Orthodox Church in the late seventeenth century, reemerging briefly in the 1920s and then again in the Gorbachev era. Since the nineteenth century, therefore, the Orthodox Church in eastern Ukraine has never played a role equivalent to that of the Catholic Church in western Ukraine.

In 1918 the Central Council (*Rada*) in Kiev declared independence from the disintegrating Russian empire, and later that year reunited with western Ukrainian territories that became stateless as a result of the collapse of the Austro-Hungarian empire. Ukrainian central control over these territories was never certain and depended on the government in power.

On the whole, Ukrainian territories were the subject of contest and armed struggle from all of Ukraine's neighbors–White Russians, Bolsheviks, Romanians (in Bessarabia and Bukovina), Poles (in Galicia and Volhynia), and Hungary (in Transcarpathia). The Bolsheviks' base of support was in the urbanized and Russified eastern Ukrainian Donbas region where they initially established an autonomous republic and then went on to found a Ukrainian Soviet Socialist Republic in the city of Kharkiv.

The 1921 Polish-Soviet Russian Treaty of Riga effectively placed the bulk of western and eastern Ukrainian territories within Poland and the USSR, respectively. Small Ukrainian enclaves were also absorbed by Czechoslovakia and Romania.

The largest national minority in interwar Poland were the 7 million Ukrainians who, although suffering various types of relatively mild discrimination, nevertheless continued to organize the Ukrainian community on a high level by maintaining the majority of the cultural, educational, and political advances made during Austrian rule.[4] The initial occupation by Soviet forces of western Ukraine in 1939–1941 led to mass deportations to Siberia and wide-scale massacres of political prisoners. At first, these Soviet crimes warmed the local population to the German invaders as well as turning the bulk of the population against Soviet rule. From 1942 until the early 1950s, western Ukraine experienced a fierce partisan struggle against Soviet power by the Organization of Ukrainian Nationalists (OUN) and Ukrainian Insurgent Army (UPA), a battle similar to those waged by nationalist partisans in the three Baltic republics.[5]

With the near total destruction of the Jewish community during World War II and the subsequent deportation of most Poles during 1945–1947, Ukrainians predominated in the urban centers of western Ukraine. In marked contrast, the urban centers of the republic's eastern regions have been Russian-speaking since the late nineteenth century.

Although the Ukrainian Catholic Church was dissolved in 1946, it continued to operate clandestinely. During the Gorbachev era, it reasserted itself as a focal point for nationalist revival in western Ukraine, a role similar to the one the Catholic Church played in Lithuania and Poland. Ukrainian Catholic parishes and assets were given to the Russian Orthodox Church after 1946. These buildings became the subject of bitter disputes between Catholics and Orthodox after the revival of the Ukrainian Catholic Church under Gorbachev.

The Ukrainian struggle for independence and the hostility that the Bolsheviks encountered in the rural areas of eastern Ukraine forced Moscow to compromise and allow some degree of autonomy during the 1920s in Soviet Ukraine. This produced a national revival in culture, rapid Ukrainianization of urban areas and the working classes, the growth of a national communist elite, and the revival of the Ukrainian Autocephalous Orthodox Church.[6] The current conflict between Ukrainian Catholics and Orthodox, as well as between two Orthodox factions, has spilled over into the political arena and even affected relations with Moscow. These factors have prevented Ukrainian Orthodoxy from acting as a "unifying force" within independent Ukraine.

By the early 1930s, with the consolidation of Joseph Stalin's rule in the USSR, the process of national revival abruptly halted. The Great Terror and artificial famine in the 1930s, which claimed an estimated 7 million lives in Ukraine, inflicted additional damage to the strength of Ukrainian national consciousness in eastern Ukraine. In that region, the cities and towns, important attributes of control in modern societies, reverted again to being dominated by a Russian-speaking population.[7]

Since the 1930s, the Soviet policy of Russification continued to retard the process of nation building and further denationalized large numbers of the Ukrainian population. In the eyes of its intelligentsia and elite, these policies endangered Ukrainians as a national community. A sense of urgency thus pervaded the Ukrainian state-building process, as did a cautiousness in dealing with national minorities owing to the lack of a wide national base committed to independence at all costs.

Lessons of the Struggle for Independence, 1917–1921

Ukraine's failure to establish an independent state in 1917–1921 plays an important role in its contemporary policy-making. What are perceived to be the mistakes of the Ukrainian government of 1917–1921? They include Ukraine's failure to build armed forces and its neglect of domestic stability and unity. In the words of Ukraine's former foreign minister Anatoliy Zlenko,

> The decision to set up Ukrainian armed forces springs not from any aggressive intent but from our tragic histo-

ry. . . . At the beginning of this century, Ukraine lost her
independence because she had declined to maintain her own
army. Bitter experience has taught us not to repeat that
mistake.[8]

The need to ensure interethnic stability and prevent social
strife are also regarded as important factors requiring careful attention in the transition period; the majority of Ukrainian democratic and nationalist groups have therefore pursued a deliberate
policy of supporting the rights of ethnic minorities. Of course,
the authorities and nationalist groups have an ulterior motive in
pursuing this policy. Granting national minorities full rights
would encourage them to speak their native tongue and no
longer regard themselves as members of the "Russian-speaking
population." In addition, granting national minorities complete
civil rights would both improve relations with Ukraine's neighbors, encouraging the latter to reciprocate toward their own
Ukrainian minority, and prevent Russia from having to take un-
due interest in defending Russians who were being discriminated
against in Ukraine.

There is also a deep fear that certain policies, such as radical
economic reform, could promote social strife. Because the major
heavy industries that would be affected by economic reform are
located in eastern Ukraine, unemployment would be largely ethnically based. Separatist tendencies could receive greater support
if eastern Ukraine were unduly affected by unemployment and
social strife. It is little wonder that economic reform is unpopular
in the Donbas, which relies heavily on inflationary credits from
Kiev for its survival. During the 1994 parliamentary elections, the
Donbas voted overwhelmingly for communist candidates.

In addition, the widespread feeling of being surrounded by
"hostile forces" harboring territorial claims has left an indelible
mark upon the Ukrainian national psyche. It has produced a
legacy of mistrust, suspicion, fear of isolation, and exaggerated
threat perceptions. Many Ukrainian authors wrongly argue that
Ukraine is the only country in the world where all of its neighbors
harbor territorial pretensions against its territory.[9]

Ukraine alone gained territory from all its central European neighbors in 1945; hanging on to these territories remains a primary task of any Kiev government. The only Ukrainian territory lost after 1945 was the Dniester Republic, which was attached to eastern Moldova (known by its Russian name of Bessarabia) to create the Moldovan Soviet Socialist Republic.

A combination of the mistakes made during previous failed attempts at gaining independence, fear of internal strife, and hanging on to diverse territories with different histories and outlooks influence the formulation of Ukrainian foreign and defense policies. A major stumbling block to the creation of a Ukrainian security policy is the absence of internal consensus over its national interests. In a manner akin to Russia and Turkey, Ukraine has at least two orientations—Western and Eurasian—as reflected in the summer 1994 presidential elections. Ukraine can therefore choose to be either on the eastern edge of Europe or the western border of Asia.

The Divided Nature of Ukrainian Society

Only after World War II ended were the bulk of Ukrainian territories—except for small enclaves in Poland, Slovakia, and Romania—incorporated within the Ukrainian Soviet Socialist Republic. Ukraine contains a vast array of regions with different histories, cultural outlooks, and levels of national consciousness. Its failure to form an independent state in modern times has prevented it from developing the ethos of a people who have united around a single idea and are prepared to endure sacrifices for life in their state. Given these factors, it is little wonder that Ukraine has no domestic consensus on security policy to require any Ukrainian leader to seek compromise.

Instead, many inhabitants of eastern-southern Ukraine look to independence only in terms of economic benefits.[10] It is unlikely, however, that a higher standard of living could in itself provide the long-term loyalty to the newly independent state that is required to maintain domestic stability and secure the legitimacy of the Ukrainian state in its current borders. The Ukrainian national psyche has been marked by a mixture of loyalties traditionally found among subject peoples in multinational empires.[11]

Kiev's hegemony within this sprawling, large territory has never been completely certain, which partly contributes to Ukraine's deep feelings of insecurity. Although the Ukrainian SSR within its present borders existed for more than half a century, it was never governed as a single unit, but as regions in a larger empire. The residents of the Donbas and Crimea looked traditionally to Moscow—not Kiev—for solace and support. These trends are growing.

Clearly, however, the newly independent Ukrainian state will be successful in maintaining control over its eastern areas only if the inhabitants of the region increasingly adopt a Ukrainian identity. A Ukrainian identity is possible in eastern Ukraine, where Russians have lived for centuries, intermarried with Ukrainians, and remain the majority ethnic group. Although many Ukrainians in eastern Ukraine are Russian speakers, their attitudes toward key issues, such as independence and the armed forces, are still likely to differ from the ethnically Russian population's. But their identity will depend upon maintaining good relations with Russia, ending the domestic political and economic crisis, and continuing its positive minority policy.

Although 51 percent of the Donbas declared itself Ukrainian in the 1989 census, together with 44 percent Russian, a recent survey gave a different picture: 32 percent Ukrainian, 27.5 percent Russian, and 36.5 percent "Russian-Ukrainian." In other words, the Donbas has a common Russian-Ukrainian cultural identity traditionally associated with border regions. This counterbalances the nationalism of western Ukraine and prevents Ukraine's withdrawing from the CIS, which would cut eastern Ukrainians away from their Russian cultural roots and lead, in their eyes, to an even greater economic decline than has hitherto taken place. In addition, eastern, unlike western-central, Ukrainians do not have an image of Russia as an imperialistic power and are thus less concerned about closer integration within the CIS.

A country that is divided over a question so fundamental as whether Russia is its best friend or worst enemy will undoubtedly find it difficult to elaborate a security policy. Any Ukrainian leader who cannot find a balance between these two mutually opposing constituencies will ultimately fail in his policy of maintaining Ukraine's territorial integrity and internal cohesion.

Eastern Ukraine is the main center for agitation in favor of federalism (one of the most heated debates in contemporary Ukraine). Although western Ukrainians continue to stereotype their eastern Ukrainian brethren as "separatists," the Donbas would only agitate for reunion with Russia if Ukraine were to disintegrate or a radical nationalist leadership were to form in Kiev.[12] The Donbas is likely to demand a separate status, as outlined in various statements and polls in 1993–1994, in order that a greater share of the state budget, to which they allegedly contribute a majority, is maintained in their region because of the ineptitude of the new center, Kiev. This is a symptom of the regional devolution taking place throughout the former USSR, including Russia.

But the ethnically Russian population of the Crimea (most of which only arrived after 1945) poses a more complicated and intractable problem that will defy quick solution because it identifies closely with Russia. The Crimea is potentially Europe's next potential flash point, which could be the spark that would lead Ukraine and Russia into full-blown conflict, as Alsace-Lorraine did between Germany and France before 1870.

The transformation of this inert, amorphous Ukrainian population (*narod*, not *natsiya*) into a civil society united by a common past and future will require time and patience. It is likely that any future nationalist government may be tempted to Ukrainianize the Russian-speaking population of eastern Ukraine (particularly through the armed forces and educational system). But the majority of Ukrainian political groups and leadership have rejected a "revolutionary" Ukrainianization (which would severely strain interethnic relations) in favor of an "evolutionary" policy, first in history and culture, rejecting language as the ultimate symbol of "patriotism." In a multiethnic society, such as Ukraine, it would be dangerous to base allegiance to the new state upon language criteria alone. Kiev, the capital city, although still largely Russian-speaking, consistently votes for Ukrainian patriotic candidates in elections. In this manner, it is not unlike Dublin, capital of Eire, which is primarily English-speaking.[13]

16

Unifying the population of Ukraine at a time when the former regime's legitimacy has disintegrated but the legitimacy of the new one has still to be established will prove to be difficult. Neither Ukrainian nationalism, religion, democracy and civil rights, or economic improvement could be used toward this end. Although rejecting the use of Ukrainian nationalism internally as leading to instability, the authorities have consequently attempted to promote Ukraine's stature, prestige, and legitimacy on the international scene. But the lack of a new state "ideology" within the Ukrainian leadership is a dangerous vacuum that hampers Ukraine in developing internal cohesion and formulating a security policy.

The Ukrainian authorities, concerned about the lack of a "unifying ideology" around which to build the new state, believe themselves to be in a position similar to the Italians in 1870 and the Poles in 1921. Educated in the former Soviet system of ideas, the Ukrainian leadership does not feel comfortable with the absence of an ideology. In the words of one author, "A state can have an army, police, be able to ensure an all penetrating political control, but if it does not possess a cemented spirit, then it is without perspective, a weak creation."[14]

Suggestions for this "national idea" have included "national democracy" and the "national-state idea." The danger is that this could spill over into exclusivist nationalism. This will inevitably mean the search for historical myths and glorious heroes, especially for the younger generation, in order to prove to a still skeptical population that Ukraine did indeed have a "glorious" past (and will therefore, have a "glorious" future).[15]

Finally, notable differences exist between eastern and western Ukraine in their attitudes to various key political, economic, and ethnic questions. An opinion poll conducted in eastern Ukraine in November 1992 pointed to greater socialist sentiments, fewer religious believers, less patriotism, greater support for authoritarian values, and less inclination to support democracy. Eastern Ukrainians were also less approving of radical political and economic changes and more disillusioned with the authorities. According to the opinion poll, the majority of eastern Ukrainians had favorable views of Russians (in contrast to western-central Ukraine, where views are similar to those found in the Baltic republics). Eastern Ukrainians are also less optimistic than western Ukrainians about the future and the chances of success of current reform programs.[16]

The regional diversity of Ukraine is thus considerable and likely to grow if the domestic political and economic crisis escalates. The mutually contradictory orientations found within Ukraine are tearing at the political fabric of the country. The success of either orientation (pro- or anti-Russian) would lead to instability, and possibly even civil war that could suck in outside powers, such as Russia, inducing them to advance their territorial designs at the expense of Ukraine. The search for compromise and consensus politics is inevitable for any Ukrainian leader.

Potential Territorial and Border Disputes

The independent Ukrainian state inherited a large number of territorial conflicts and disputes that play a role in developing the contemporary threat perceptions outlined in later chapters. Before World War II, territories with Ukrainian ethnographic majorities were divided between its neighbors and the source of various sharp disputes over the "historical," ethnic, and political rights to these lands. At one time or another, therefore, Ukraine's borders have been contested by all of its neighbors, except Belarus. A small number of Ukrainian national minorities live in Poland, Slovakia, Romania, Moldova, and Belarus, where they all live contiguous to the Ukrainian border, except in the case of Poland.

The only major territorial threats lie first and foremost with Russia and next with Romania. In the Russian case the threat is made all the more dangerous because of the large number of Russians and denationalized Ukrainians living in Ukraine, the Crimean question, and the dangerous belief within the Russian leadership that Ukrainian independence is "temporary." Russian security policy has shifted steadily to the right during 1992–1995, becoming in the process more assertive in supporting its coethnics abroad and reestablishing its hegemony within the former USSR.[17]

Although 11 million Russians live in Ukraine, 7 million Ukrainians also live in the Russian Federation. Russian complaints about forcible "Ukrainianization" are increasingly matched by Ukrainian claims that their coethnics in Russia are also denied minority rights. Areas adjacent to Ukraine within Russia, such as the Kuban area of the northern Caucasus (home to the Russian Black Sea Fleet and energy port of Novorossisk), are regarded as "Ukrainian ethnographic territories" for historical and ethnic reasons. If the disintegration of the Russian Federation were to take place, a nationalist Ukrainian government might be tempted to annex these adjacent areas to Ukraine. Alternatively, the disintegration of Ukraine could lead to the secession of eastern Ukraine and the Crimea to Russia.

Russian territorial conflicts rest with Ukraine over eastern Ukraine (Donbas), southern Ukraine (so-called *Novorossiya*, the Tsarist term meaning New Russia), and the Crimea. In all of these regions, only the Crimea has a Russian majority that moved there after World War II when the Tatars were deported and their autonomous republic abolished.

Since 1954 the Crimea has been a part of Ukraine and until December 1990 held the status of a county (*oblast*). In January 1991 the Crimea was elevated to the status of an autonomous republic within Ukraine, and in spring-summer 1992 it concluded negotiations with Ukraine over the sharing of power between Kiev and the Crimea. The Crimean republican elite has therefore a great deal of autonomy within which to pursue its agendas.

The Crimea's declaration of independence in early May 1992 seemed less an attempt to break away from Ukraine than a bargaining chip in its negotiations with Kiev over the separation of power. After all, the former national communist leadership, which held power under Nikolai Bagrov and supported the August 1991 coup d'etat, had more in common with Kravchuk than with Yeltsin. Although Ukraine successfully defused the situation in the Crimea by granting it a high degree of autonomy, Ukrainian and Russian nationalists are not content with the situation for different reasons. The Crimean leadership could be attracted by a post-Yeltsin nationalist/communist Russia or concerned by a post-Kravchuk nationalist Ukraine. These trends were sharply exacerbated by the election of Yuriy Meshkov as Crimean president, leader of the Russia bloc, in January 1994. The post of Crimean president was abolished in March 1995.

Aside from Ukraine, the only republic of the former USSR where Ukrainians outnumber Russians is Moldova. The Dniester Republic has been the scene of ethnic and political conflict with the Moldovan authorities since 1990, primarily over its refusal to grant it autonomy and the campaign for early reunification with Romania. The Dniester Republic was a part of Ukrainian SSR territory before World War II and historically never belonged to Romania. Romanian and Moldovan nationalists have thus suggested that it be exchanged for Northern Bukovina (currently Chernivtsi oblast), which Ukraine obtained from Romania as a consequence of the Molotov-Ribbentrop Pact. Ukrainian-Romanian relations will continue to remain poor as long as extreme nationalists harboring territorial demands remain in power in Bucharest. Ukrainian-Russian relations will also remain strained in the case of the Dniester Republic, where Ukraine opposes the dismemberment of Moldova.

Ukrainian minorities lived within the Hungarian state and later in the Hungarian portion of the Austro-Hungarian empire in Transcarpathia and eastern Slovakia. These territories were removed from Hungary and given to the Czechoslovak state in the interwar period. Transcarpathia, although geographically located in western Ukraine, has made demands for autonomy that have been resisted thus far by Kiev. Potentially, Hungary and Slovakia could lay claim to part or all of Transcarpathia.

The history of Polish-Ukrainian relations is dominated by conflict at least since the seventeenth century. After the disintegration of the Austrian-Hungarian empire in 1918, Poland's attempts to reconstitute itself within its "historic" borders exercised little regard for the rights of ethnic minorities who lived there. The large discontented Ukrainian minority in Poland pursued their demands either through parliament or through acts of terrorism by Ukrainian nationalist groups.

During World War II, a Polish-Ukrainian civil war erupted again in western Ukraine. Between 1945 and 1947, the Polish inhabitants of western Ukraine, which was incorporated within the Ukrainian SSR, were deported to Poland. It was ostensibly to stop the struggle of Ukrainian nationalist partisans in southeastern Poland that the Ukrainian population was deported from the region to the newly acquired German territories in 1947. The bloody conflicts of the interwar period and the 1940s left a bitter legacy that had to be initially overcome before relations could improve between both countries.

During the 1980s, the Solidarity movement in Poland, certain emigré publications, and Ukrainian opposition groups helped to overcome historical animosities and focus on current political and strategic questions. Relations between Ukraine and Poland are now good, and the likelihood of territorial conflict between them is therefore remote.

Conclusion

The historical legacy of hundreds of years of external domination coupled with more than seven decades of Soviet totalitarianism has left a great scar upon the Ukrainian national psyche. This has produced sharp regional differences and outlooks, a major cleavage between western-central and eastern-southern Ukraine, and varying degrees of national consciousness.

A lack of statehood in modern times, large national minorities, and a lack of experience in dealing with the outside world have produced a deep sense of insecurity within the Ukrainian ruling elite. This insecurity is translated into suspicion, mistrust, and exaggerated threat perceptions. Regional disparities and varying degrees of national consciousness influence the ability to forge a coherent security policy and formulate generally accepted national interests.

The requirement of building a Ukrainian identity among denationalized Ukrainians and national minorities who would be loyal to Kiev will therefore preoccupy Ukrainian leaders. Ukrainian governments will be tempted to reverse the legacy of denationalization, the speed of which will depend on who is in power in Kiev. Yet opinion polls show that a majority of Ukrainian citizens are opposed to border changes, which they fear could lead to wider conflicts. The gradual legitimization of the Ukrainian state is likely to take place in eastern Ukraine if the economic crisis is overcome. If it is not, and nationalists take power in Kiev, the growth of separatism within eastern Ukraine and Crimea cannot be ruled out. If this were to transpire, Russia would be inevitably sucked into the conflict on behalf of ethnic Russians, especially in the Crimean Republic.

Ukraine has been successful in maintaining interethnic peace. But the Crimea and the Dniester Republic of Moldova, given their particular histories, will continue to be potentially destabilizing areas that could bring Ukraine (and Moldova) into conflict with Russia. The Crimea, in particular, is a potential flash point that could ignite a major Russian-Ukrainian conflict. A conflict in the Crimea also has the potential to drag in Turkey because of the Tatar demands to renew their autonomous republic on the peninsula.

Ukraine's failure to establish an independent state in 1917–1921 highly influences current Ukrainian policy-making. This legacy is reflected in the priority given today to building the armed forces and maintaining domestic social and ethnic stability. Ukraine's struggle for independence was a simultaneous struggle against most of its neighbors who, at one time or another, have harbored territorial claims against it. The current Ukrainian borders were only created after 1945; the potential for border conflicts therefore remain large, primarily with Romania and Russia. Were Ukraine to disintegrate, other neighboring powers might also be tempted to advance their territorial claims in a repeat of the events of 1917–1921. Certainly, there are many similarities between the domestic political and economic crises of 1917–1918 and 1993–1994, where "the leadership has lost faith in its ability to properly manage the country."[18]

Ukraine, given the historical record of territorial changes and claims by the majority of its neighbors, is likely to remain a status quo power in central and eastern Europe. There is a broad consensus within Ukraine against territorial changes and a deep fear that any loss of one region of its territory would have a domino effect, leading to the ultimate disintegration of the entire state. The demands for Russian naval basing rights in Sevastopol should be looked at by Western policymakers with this in mind. The Ukrainian leadership will react in an exaggerated manner and with a certain degree of paranoia to border claims by foreign powers.

The return of part, or all, of Ukraine to Russian dependence or the arrival to power of a nationalist strongman in either Kiev or Moscow (or both) would presage conflict. The degree of suppressed dislike for Russia in western-central Ukraine is sufficiently high among a majority of Ukrainians. The country possesses no Russian military bases (apart from Sevastopol) and has large security forces that would not need to search on the international arms market for supplies. Although not all of the security forces could be relied upon in the event of conflict with Russia, sufficient numbers would still exist to make any civil war or conflict far more severe than in Bosnia-Herzegovina. For European security, therefore, the stakes are much higher of encouraging positive domestic and foreign policies by Ukraine.

2

Domestic Sources
of Security Policy

This chapter analyzes the domestic sources of Ukrainian security policy, with particular emphasis on surveying the main policymakers and origins and formulation of Ukrainian security policy. This will include parliament, president, elite, public opinion, and civil-military relations.

Ukrainian independence could not have been achieved in December 1991 without the help of the national communists. At that time, their interests coincided with the interests of their nationalist allies. Although the national communists played an important short-term role in ensuring social and ethnic stability, their continued domination of the ruling elite and levers of power blocked Ukraine's program of political and economic reform and led to economic stagnation.

As Ukrainian instability has grown, social and national consensus has broken down, and the ruling elite has divided over different orientations. These factors profoundly affect Ukrainian security policy. It is difficult to reorient the loyalties of Ukraine's citizens and national minorities to a Ukrainian state that appears economically and politically unappealing and unstable. The growing crisis has encouraged regionalism and pro-Russian tendencies. All these factors have undermined the legitimacy of the state, in turn preventing the formulation of a coherent security policy with broad public consensus.

Ukraine's leaders did not sufficiently recognize the domestic threats to Ukrainian security. Yet the economic crisis, corruption, lack of political reform, and entrenchment of influential communist groups are as great, or even greater, a threat to the survival of the Ukrainian state as potential foreign threats.

In fact, a wide gulf exists between threats that genuinely endanger Ukrainian security and threats that are exaggerated and grow out of the Ukrainian leadership's insecurity. In addition, to distract attention from the domestic threats to Ukrainian independence, Ukraine's leadership has, to some extent, played the nationalist card by blaming Russia for its economic crisis. The growing domestic crisis has permitted Russia to apply even greater external pressure on Ukraine in its weakened position.

The Role of Key Groups

The Ukrainian Elite

The resurgence and abiding strength of national communism within the ruling class in Ukraine during the late Gorbachev era is not an unusual phenomenon (unlike the situation in neighboring Belarus, where no tradition of national communism exists).[1] National communism had previously appeared in Ukraine during the 1920s and 1960s, when it demanded greater cultural, linguistic, and economic rights as well as the decentralization of the USSR into a confederation.[2] But these periods of national communism had always been followed by repression during the 1930s and 1970s.

It may be argued that if Mikhail Gorbachev had proposed a confederal solution to the Ukrainian communist elite before the August 1991 coup d'etat, Leonid Kravchuk would have accepted it.[3] On no occasion before August 1991 did Kravchuk, then chairman of the Ukrainian parliament and leader of the national communist wing of the Communist Party of Ukraine (CPU), propose independence. Kravchuk could not have helped but take notice that his popularity rating rose dramatically after September 1990 when he became chairman of the Ukrainian parliament and began to champion Ukrainian sovereignty. Between November 1990 and April 1991, Kravchuk moved from twenty-first position to that of Ukraine's most popular politician by promoting "sovereignty."[4] Ukraine's national communists have always tended to historically prefer confederation and sovereignty to full independence; thus many of them cannot perceive of Ukraine's future as lying outside the Commonwealth of Independent States (CIS).

Stagnation, political and economic conservatism, mutual protection of the old boy network, and clannish ties are the hallmark of the national communists, who have been termed Ukraine's largest political force or "party of power" (*partia vlada*). They lack any ideology and are pragmatic, representing the "inner party" of the former CPU, which controls the state apparatus, media, and economy, and possessed a majority of deputies within parliament. Their most striking characteristic is their amorphousness; they have no program aside from their desire to be accepted as true "Europeans" and "democrats," to be all things to all men. Their views constantly shift, depending on the prevailing mood and balance of forces. This lack of consistency– their hallmark– reflects their constantly changing attitudes toward nuclear weapons, the West, and the CIS.[5]

Of the six presidential candidates in December 1991 (two of whom were Russian, but all of whom supported independence), only one represented the *ancien* regime–Leonid Kravchuk. He garnered more than 60 percent of the vote, while the noncommunist candidates foolishly divided their vote among five candidates. The only region where Kravchuk came second place was western Ukraine, where he was beaten by Viacheslav Chornovil. Kravchuk's election thus reflected Ukraine's deep regional divisions, divergent attitudes toward Russia, and uneven degrees of national consciousness.

Former president Kravchuk's popularity plummeted in 1993–1994. He was unpopular in different regions for many reasons–patriotic, economic, and political. He was perceived as either too, or not enough, pro-Russian. Whether noncommunist groups have sufficient forces and popularity at their disposal to completely oust the *ancien* regime is unlikely. In many postcommunist countries in central-eastern Europe, including economically prosperous Poland, instability has combined with economic hardship to return reformed communists to power. Ukrainian national communists have neither formed a radical nationalist party (as in Serbia, Romania, and Slovakia) or become social democrats (as in Poland, Lithuania, and Hungary).

The accent on centrism that Kravchuk used to promote national consensus and keep the country together, while failing economically, largely contained ethnic and social stability. To remove this centrist force because the crisis is growing would severely damage national consensus and greatly increase domestic strife.

Political Parties and Civil Society

The lack of democratic traditions in most Ukrainian territories formerly under Russian sovereignty impedes the establishment of a parliamentary democracy in Ukraine. Only western Ukraine, with its different, more liberal legacy of foreign rule, and such large cities as Kiev and Kharkiv have a civil society, vibrant independent press, and strong political parties similar to those found in the Baltic republics. The incipient weakness of political parties and the embryonic state of civil society throughout Ukraine also create the conditions that could lead to authoritarianism or the demand for a "strong hand."

A state based on the rule of law is still "not firmly rooted" in Ukraine and the implementation of laws in the democratic transformation of society were "erratic." In the words of the U.S. Commission on Security and Cooperation in Europe, "Totalitarianism has passed in Ukraine; it is not clear whether authoritarianism has as well," while "democracy is still fragile."[6] Post-Soviet republics, such as Ukraine, lack the social building blocks necessary to ensure their early transformation into democratic systems and market economies.[7] The decision-making process and division of power between the executive and legislative branches remain confused, preventing disciplined government and a clear division of responsibilities.

The influence of political parties within Ukraine is still small. Political parties were formed in Ukraine during two waves in 1990–1991 and 1992–1993. They still remain confined to large

cities, except in western Ukraine, where they are found in rural
and local areas. Small towns and rural areas, on the whole, have
either no or few members of political parties. National-
democratic parties, such as the Ukrainian Popular Movement
(Rukh) and the Republican Party, tend to be stronger in western-
central Ukraine while socialist, liberal, and communist parties
are more strongly based in the eastern-southern regions of the
republic. There are few groups with an all-Ukrainian base and
appeal.

Role of the President

Presidential elections were held in Ukraine on December 1, 1991,
the same day as the independence referendum, and in June-July
1994. Of the six presidential candidates in December 1991, the
only one from the *ancien* regime, Leonid Kravchuk, was then
chairman of the Ukrainian parliament. In the summer 1994 presidential elections, four of the six candidates were from the *ancien*
regime; one was a businessman with close ties to the *ancien* regime, while Volodymyr Lanavyi represented the liberal, reformist
camp. All nationalist hopes were therefore pinned on Kravchuk.
    Initially the democrats welcomed presidential representatives
as a means to dismantle the Soviet system, but found that Kravchuk was more interested in using them as a means to consolidate
the hold of the "Party of Power" over local affairs. It was more a
case of "business as usual," of relying on old cadres, than revolutionary change. As one commentator put it: "Mr. Kravchuk is
replacing elected regional councils with old communist *apparat-
chiks*. They have a new title ('prefects,' not party secretaries) and
a new allegiance (the president, not the politburo), but the faces
are almost unchanged."[8]
    Meanwhile, parliament continued to weaken the presi-
dency, which it regarded as a threat to its monopoly of power,
especially at the local level. The president's powers were weakened by parliamentary veto over presidential decrees and elimination of the post of vice president. Parliament rejected proposals
to consolidate presidential rule by allowing the executive to head
the government and determine its members.

Former president Kravchuk failed to articulate a clear vision in his position as leader of Ukraine and fluctuated and embraced different concepts and orientations at different times. This was particularly the case during 1992 when a large endorsement for independence and postindependence euphoria, when communist or pro-Russian groups were either banned or unorganized, could have been utilized to promote economic and political reform.

The presidency of Ukraine was won by a representative of the second tier of the communist party *nomenklatura*, an advocate of compromise. This ensured that his role would be one of national integration "rather than as the main element in the formation and implementation of a specific political course for the executive branch."[9] Kravchuk's balancing act between the government and democratic opposition, some of whom were coopted in the presidential Duma, removed him from direct responsibility and allowed him to maintain a high degree of popularity. But, at the same time, it deprived him of articulating a clearly defined position and leadership role. His aloofness from the government merely increased his dependency on the *ancien* regime.

Coopting the *ancien* regime to independence was successful, unlike in many other post-Soviet states, but the price of their appeasement—"business as usual"—only served to produce the illusion of short-term stability. This policy may have been useful in ensuring domestic stability in 1992, but the weaknesses evident in Kravchuk's lack of leadership, indecisiveness, and failure to articulate a vision were plainly evident between 1993 and 1994.

The law on the elections of local councils and heads of councils foresees the creation of new local and regional executive bodies that replaced the system of presidential prefects in summer 1994. Although this is a positive step to eliminate the executive power conflict in 1992-1994. At the same time, at a time of growing regionalism, the elimination of presidential prefects could weaken Ukraine's territorial cohesion. President Leonid Kuchma, who favors strong executive power, has in the absence of presidential prefects been forced to coopt local councils under his authority. Parliament has backed the creation of strong executive power that Kuchma demanded to implement reform.

Ukrainian Parliament and Policymakers

The voting patterns in the March 1990 and 1994 republican elections reflected the regional and historical cleavages within Ukraine outlined in chapter 1. Western-central Ukraine, especially Galicia and Kiev, voted for noncommunist candidates whereas eastern and southern Ukraine voted for conservatives and liberal reformers.

After the December 1991 referendum on independence, the "People's Council" and Rukh divided primarily over their attitudes toward cooperation with national communists. Former president Kravchuk argued that, to avoid repeating the 1917–1921 mistake of failing to achieve independence, Ukrainians should rally around him "in the interests of national unity." In this manner, Kravchuk could argue that opposition to him was therefore "unpatriotic."

Consequently, a large number of Rukh intellectuals, together with center-right political parties, who later grouped into the Congress of National Democratic Forces, adopted a "statist" program and gave unqualified support to Kravchuk. The majority of Rukh rank-and-file members grouped themselves around Viacheslav Chornovil, former long-term prisoner of conscience who opposed the "Party of Power." During 1992-1994, Chornovil, as leader of Rukh, became the focal point of continued anticommunist opposition to Kravchuk, whom they accused of usurping Ukrainian independence.

The influence of parliament has grown considerably (but not necessarily for the better) since the first election in March 1990. Not only have parliamentarians become relatively more professional, they have a clearer appreciation of their power in enacting laws and blocking the passage of legislation or ratification of treaties and documents signed by the president and government bodies. Unfortunately, little of the accumulated experience of the 1990-1994 parliament passed over into the current one, which contains less than 15 percent of the former deputies.

The formulation of foreign policy is primarily divided between three competing groups–parliamentary committees (previously dominated by nationalists and democrats but now largely controlled by communists), the Ministry of Foreign Affairs (dominated by moderate, seasoned diplomats), and presidential advisers on foreign affairs. A number of "think tanks" have also developed to assist in formulating security policy–for example, the National Institute for Strategic Studies, which was carved out of the Academy of Sciences to provide advice to the president, and the National Security Council. The Ministry of Defense has also established the Centre for Operational and Strategic Studies to develop military strategy and analyze threat perceptions.

Of these, undoubtedly the parliamentary committees have the greatest influence because they can block any agreements that the president or foreign minister sign in their individual capacity. At the same time, the parliamentary committee on foreign affairs and Foreign Ministry share a majority of common views, which allows them to cooperate to a greater degree in formulating foreign policy (not the case between the economic reform committee and government economic ministries, where a wide gulf exists). The only source of tension would be between seasoned diplomats and the perceived lack of experience of literati and former political prisoners who previously headed the parliamentary committees.

National Security Council

The National Security Council (NSC) unites defense, foreign affairs, and security service ministers, among others; but its function and role in the formulation of Ukrainian security policy is still unclear. A major reason for this is the lack of consensus within the Ukrainian leadership over national interests. The NSC was established by presidential decree on July 1, 1992, and has six permanent members (president, state adviser on national security, prime minister, chairman of the Security Service, defense and foreign ministers). Other members, with less than full voting rights, include the ministers of health, environment, internal affairs, the president of the Academy of Sciences, and the chairmen of the National Bank and State Committee on Security of State Borders.

The main task of the NSC is to advise and consult on all aspects of policy dealing with national security in the broadest sense. The NSC also coordinates and integrates different departments whose sphere of activities come under the domain of national security. Because the deliberations and decisions reached by the NSC are rarely made public, it is difficult to analyze its importance and role in policy formulation.[10] The NSC is still in the process of formation, so its role is likely to expand in the future under President Kuchma, who has restructured it into a more cohesive body.

Civil-Military Relations

The officers who agreed to take the Ukrainian oath of loyalty after January 1992 did so for many reasons, some patriotic, some socioeconomic (motivated by housing, family, and pension matters, as well as the desire for a better climate, fear of unemployment, etc.). These officers supported either energetically or passively the creation of Ukrainian armed forces; their ultimate loyalty to Ukrainian independence is of concern to Ukraine's leadership.[11] In one (probably unrepresentative) opinion poll, only 8 percent of officers in a Kiev military academy admitted that they would defend Ukraine in the event of a Russian military conflict. Although opinion polls are notoriously unreliable in the former USSR, nevertheless the Ukrainian leadership has to take into account that a proportion of their officer corps are potentially unreliable from a security point of view (especially in the event of military conflict with Russia).

The major vehicle that promoted a nationalistic cleansing of the armed forces was the Union of Ukrainian Officers (UUO), which has links to Rukh and other nationalist groups. Its influence is greatest in the Socio-Psychological Department of the Ministry of Defense, where it conducts a policy of Ukrainianization, and on the attestation boards of the Ministry of Defense, where it can weed out suspect, "unpatriotic" officers.[12] Many critics have accused it of being a "new political party" within the armed forces, taking upon itself the same responsibilities as the former communist party.[13] The UUO has repeatedly complained of the large numbers of Russians in the higher echelons of the Ukrainian armed forces, which the Ministry of Defense claims is necessary because of the lack of qualified Ukrainians for those posts.

The Ukrainian leadership meanwhile finds the UUO indispensable, regarding its officers as its most "loyal" support; it can be no coincidence that nationalists have been given key posts within the intelligence apparatus. The UUO is active within leading positions of the newly created military intelligence service (whose main activity is undoubtedly directed against Russia), the Department to Combat Corruption and Organized Crime and Department to Defend National Statehood and Society[14] within the Security Service. If anything, the influence of the UUO is likely to increase greatly; its influence is taken into account by the Ukrainian leadership (former defense minister Konstantin Morozov attended all of their congresses) when it raises issues such as nuclear weapons and the Black Sea Fleet.[15]

In July 1993 military intelligence was reorganized; the Main Directorate of Military Intelligence was created from two existing structures to take military counterintelligence away from the Security Service. The appointed head of this new structure is Major-General Oleksandr Skipalskyi, leader of the UUO and a supporter of Rukh. This is clearly an attempt by Ukraine's leadership to obtain independent intelligence information from sources believed to be more patriotic and an alternative to the Security Service (which has many former KGB personnel).[16]

The activities of the armed and security forces in Ukraine are set to grow as the politicians seem unable to solve the country's domestic crisis. If Ukraine were faced with the same kind of Russian-backed separatism and domestic strife as in Georgia, or deadlock occurred between its executive and legislative branches as in Russia, the suspension of parliament and creation of the post of an authoritarian leader could not be ruled out (especially with the election of the more abrasive President Kuchma, whose program of economic reform will clash with the communist lobby in parliament). This could only be undertaken with the support of the armed and security forces. Public opinion is increasingly supportive of a "strong hand," a post that former president Kravchuk would have been unable to fit into comfortably (unlike President Kuchma).

Morozov resigned as Ukraine's defense minister on October 4, 1993, after serving in this post since September 3, 1991.[17] Morozov stated that he did not want the armed forces "dragged into political games." His decision came in the wake of the polarized political situation in Ukraine's parliament and the tense events in Moscow and in protest at the decisions reached at the Massandra summit over the Black Sea Fleet and Sevastopol. On September 21, the Ukrainian parliament had voted no confidence in the Kuchma government, reducing Morozov to only acting minister of defense.

Morozov's replacement as defense minister was General Vitaliy Radetskyi, a Ukrainian born in 1944 in Cherkasy oblast, central Ukraine.[18] Radetskyi joined the Soviet armed forces in 1968. One of his last posts was as the commander of the Sixth Tank Division of the Soviet Army. Between 1989 and 1991 he was deputy commander of the Carpathian Military District and in May 1991 was promoted to a leading command post in the Odesa Military District. He is a graduate of the Kiev Military Academy, the Frunze Military Academy, and the General Staff Academy. In April 1992 Radetskyi became deputy defense minister and from January 27, 1992, served as commander of the southern operational command (formerly Odesa military district).

President Kuchma quickly replaced the defense and foreign ministers that he inherited who were staunchly loyal to his predecessor. Valeriy Shmarov was made defense minister, the first civilian to head this post in the CIS. It not only reflected Kuchma's intention of establishing personal control over the "Power Ministries," the majority of whom had undoubtedly voted for his rival Kravchuk, but also reflected his program of political and economic reform. Unlike in Russia, where the military appear out of control in the "Near Abroad" and during the Chechnya crisis, President Kuchma aims to ensure that the security forces are completely under civilian control. Shmarov is also from the military-industrial complex, as is Kuchma, and his appointment reflects the view of the ascendancy of this sector in current economic strategy.

Conflicting Nationalistic Impulses[19]

Although former president Kravchuk successfully maintained ethnic and social stability from 1992 until mid-1994, he failed to utilize this crucial period to build a pro-Western national consensus while adopting political and economic reform (unlike President Boris Yeltsin). Indeed, throughout his term in office, Kravchuk lacked any vision as to where he wanted to lead the country — hence, his constant maneuvering and changing of policies.

Pro-Russian and communist political constituencies did not form to lobby for a more pro-Russian orientation until winter 1992–1993. For at least a year, Ukraine lacked internal opposition toward moving the country geopolitically westward away from the Russian sphere of influence and introducing a reform program. Thus was missed an opportunity to break with the Soviet past, using the large mandates offered to the president and the cause of independence.

Nationalistic Orientation

The nationalists and national communists are united by a common hostility toward Russia. Kravchuk, like the nationalists, was hostile to federalization and sympathetic to the French unitarian state structure. He also supported the nationalist demand to search for new security ties in central Europe, especially as Ukraine is highly unlikely to sign the CIS Treaty on Collective Security, unlike neighboring Belarus.[20] Hence, Ukraine's proposals for a Zone of Security and Cooperation in central Europe aimed to both satisfy the domestic nationalist lobby and balance Ukraine's integration within the Russian-dominated CIS.[21]

But the nationalists are losing the struggle with public opinion, which is coming to favor reintegration and the CIS as the domestic crisis deepens and Ukraine's leadership falters in finding a solution to it. Therefore, although the majority of nationalistic Ukrainian political parties and movements support secession from the CIS, only a minority of the public would actually agree with this move (reflecting the aloofness of many political groups from the population at large). At the same time, President Kuchma is acutely aware that political-military integration with Russia or the CIS would be met by stiff domestic opposition; hence he has only proposed increasing economic integration.

The national communists are ambivalent about the CIS but appear to be moving toward a more pragmatic view of economic integration within the CIS. Although nationalistic groups have tolerated (but disliked) Ukrainian membership of the CIS, they would be vehemently hostile to Kiev's signing the CIS Charter or becoming a full member of the CIS Economic Union.

A more uncompromising anti-Russian/CIS position is growing within the radical right political spectrum, particularly the Ukrainian National Assembly (UNA). The UNA has a paramilitary wing, the Ukrainian People's Self Defence Forces (UNSO), which has undertaken military action in Georgia against the Abkhazians, in the Dniester Republic against the Moldovans, and in Chechnya against the Russians. With upwards of 10,000 members and 3 in parliament, their brand of integral nationalism is likely to gain popularity if the economic crisis grows, Russian pressure continues, and a real "pro-Russian" president is elected.[22]

Pro-Russian and CIS Groups

The December 1991 referendum produced an overwhelming majority: 90 percent favored independence (76 percent of those eligible to vote), even in regions with large concentrations of Russians, such as the Donbas. But the lowest numbers of votes for independence of those eligible to vote, representing less than two-thirds of the vote, was made in 4 eastern-southern counties (where a quarter of the Ukrainian population lives)—Donets'k, Luhans'k, Kharkiv, and Odesa—and in the Crimea, where it was as low as 36.5 percent (54 percent of those who voted). These areas are the likely sources of future territorial dispute with Russia and could, in certain circumstances, secede from Ukraine.

Since winter 1992, areas with large Russian minorities, such as the Donbas and Crimea, have spawned new political parties and organizations with a different orientation than the nationalist and democratic parties that helped sweep Ukraine to independence in 1987–1991.

The Ukrainian Union of Industrialists and Entrepreneurs (UUIE), who strongly support close economic ties with Russia, dominated the government in 1993-1994 to appease eastern Ukrainian sentiment and balance nationalist domination of foreign and defense policy portfolios. The UUIE has established a Party of Labour and works closely with the Inter-Regional Association of Industrialists (IRAI). The IRAI meanwhile groups together 80 to 90 percent of the industrial directors from five eastern Ukrainian counties and finances separatist political structures in the Donbas region.

Ukrainian nationalist groups have little influence and few branches in the Donbas. New Ukraine is only influential within certain areas of eastern Ukraine where there is a large number of technical intelligentsia (such as the city of Kharkiv). In contrast, the greatest support for economic reform is in western Ukraine and such large cities as Kiev.

Support is lowest in eastern Ukraine, which lacks an intelligentsia to articulate support for it. Also, its working classes fear the impact of privatization upon primary and antiquated industries. The New Ukraine bloc, the main engine promoting economic reform in Ukraine, has faced difficulties in increasing its popular base in eastern Ukraine, its primary location. This has undoubtedly been a major factor limiting the domestic pressure for economic reform. During the 1994 parliamentary elections the Inter-Regional Bloc of Reforms (IRBR), led by Kuchma, failed to make inroads into the Donbas, which elected communists. In December 1994, the IRBR and New Ukraine united into a party strongly committed to reform and President Kuchma.

Regional or separatist groups (Intermovement, Civic Congress, Democratic Movement of the Donbas), pro-Russian "Red Director" lobbies, and revived communist and socialist groups dominate the political landscape of the Donbas. The Donbas political and economic elite act as a pressure group promoting Ukraine's full membership in the CIS Economic Union and closer, friendlier relations with Russia. Only the Liberal Party, based in Donets'k, is pro-Western in its orientation and economic program (although it failed to score successes in the 1994 elections).

The Donbas and eastern Ukrainian vote (40 percent of the electorate) is primarily divided between these groups whose views on Ukrainian independence are either lukewarm or hostile. The demand to add a third question on Donbas autonomy and Russian-Ukrainian bilingual state languages was reportedly a major factor in dissuading the Ukrainian parliament from holding the September 1993 referendum.[23] Regional self-government is supported by 64 percent of Donbas residents, while 7 percent are even ready to undertake "civil disobedience and military actions" if their demands are not met for autonomy. These trends are likely to continue unless the crisis is halted and relations with Russia are improved (both priority areas for President Kuchma).[24]

The parliamentary elections in spring-summer 1994 pointed to the growing pro-Russian trends in Ukraine. Former chairman of the Security Service Yeshen Marchuk argued that "the problem of the Crimea and of regionalism as a whole as one of those threats which is of prime importance to Ukraine owing to economic, historic and other reasons."[25] Two key Donbas oblasts bordering Russia – Donets'k and Luhans'k – provide 60 of the deputies to the Ukrainian parliament, or 13.3 percent of the total of 450 deputies. The majority of the communist-socialist deputies elected to the new parliament are based in these counties.[26]

The two Donbas oblast councils held simultaneous opinion polls during the 1994 elections (Kravchuk had persuaded them to refrain, as in the Crimea, from holding referendums that would be legally binding). These polls asked whether the new Ukrainian constitution should include references to Russian as the second state language and Ukraine as a federalized state. Both of these questions obtained high endorsements of 87.1 percent and 79.7 percent respectively. The third question asked whether voters agreed with the view that Russian should be utilized as a second state language alongside Ukrainian in their two oblasts, while the final question asked voters whether Ukraine should become a full member of the CIS Economic Union and the Inter-Parliamentary Assembly, as well as a signatory to its Charter. Both of these questions obtained 89 percent and 88.7 percent endorsements as well.[27]

Crimea

The election of the pro-Russian separatist president Yuriy Meshkov in January 1994 upset Kiev's plans and set alarm bells ringing
in Kiev.[28] The Ukrainian parliament then proceeded to issue an
ultimatum to the Crimean leadership to abide by the Ukrainian
laws and constitution, claiming that the Crimea had no right to
conduct its own foreign, defense, or monetary policies. President
Meshkov ignored this ultimatum and brought in a Russian citi-
zen to be his new premier. He has also demanded the withdrawal
of Ukrainian military formations, arguing that the Black Sea Fleet
would ensure the peninsula's security.

President Meshkov originally flirted with the idea of a referendum on secession, but then dropped it in favor of a poll on
parliamentary election day. "The poll will not have the force of
law. This is just a consultation with the people, which will give
us backing for further action," said Meshkov's spokesman. The
reasons why President Meshkov backed down from his campaign
pledge to take the Crimea out of Ukraine are threefold. First, the
Russian leadership reacted cautiously to the latest developments
in the Crimea. Premier Viktor Chernomyrdin told Kiev that
"Ukraine need not fear that Russia's position will change."[29] Russia is less interested in annexing the Crimea, which would curtail
Ukraine's pledge to denuclearize and bring U.S. condemnation
and support for Ukrainian territorial integrity. Second, the current Russian leadership is more likely to utilize the Crimea as a
pressure point to make Kiev more amenable to Russian demands
for closer reintegration (in the manner of Abkhazia and the
Dniester Republic). Third, as the former Crimean premier Yev-
geniy Saburov admitted, the Crimea could not survive without
Ukrainian subsidies. The bulk of its foodstuffs, energy, and fresh
water come from Ukraine. Sevastopol obtains 90 percent of its
budget from Kiev.

Crimean president Meshkov went ahead with his own opinion poll despite threats from Kiev, adding a call to boycott the
Ukrainian parliamentary elections by taking away the ballot papers. The poll asked Crimean residents whether they supported
the right to dual citizenship, whether presidential decrees should
have the force of law, and whether relations between the Crimea

and Ukraine should be regulated by a treaty and agreement (similar to that between Tatarstan and Moscow).[30] Both Meshkov's spokesman and former president Kravchuk reiterated that the poll would not have the force of law, although the issue was later further clouded by the claim that the results would determine Meshkov's policies.

Both parliament and president issued a strong resolution and decree.[31] Kravchuk's strongly worded decree stated that the poll was unconstitutional and inconsistent with Ukrainian legislation. Kravchuk's former political adviser Mykola Mikhailchenko added that "the president can take all the constitutional means to make sure it is fulfilled." He then warned, "We can no longer make concessions to separatists in the Crimea–their goals could lead to an Abkhazian solution. It is better to stop the separatists now rather than having to restore order later by military means."[32] Ukraine has doubled the size of its security force (army, navy, national guard, and border troops) presence in the Crimea since December 1991 to an estimated 52,000, a figure slightly higher than the 48,000-strong Black Sea Fleet.

Former president Kravchuk's military option would have been a last resort, particularly after digesting the Georgian de facto loss of sovereignty as a consequence of its Abkhaz blunders.[33] He therefore talked of other means, particularly economic-energy pressure: "Let's speak frankly, Crimea today is a region which is subsidized by Ukraine. We don't have to go into all the figures, there's energy, water, etc. As the Russian saying goes, don't try to wear clothes that don't fit." The Crimea is the largest defaulter on nonpayment of energy, and Kiev therefore has cut electricity supplies by one third.

The largest faction in the new Crimean parliament is the Russia Bloc, with two-thirds of seats (54 out of 94), the main backer of Meshkov. The communists obtained 11 percent and the Party of Economic Revival of the Crimea 7 percent. But Meshkov's popularity dramatically declined, a prime reason for which is his inability to fulfill economic promises made during the presidential elections and conflict with Kiev.[34] In March 1995, Kiev abolished the post of Crimean president, which did not lead to widespread opposition on the peninsula.

The main Ukrainian and Tatar organizations on the peninsula have joined forces with the latter vowing to preserve Ukrainian territorial integrity.[35] The Crimean Tatar National Movement and its "parliament" (*Majlis*) are supported by Turkey, where an estimated 1 to 3 million Tatars live. The Tatars are also backed by the Confederation of Caucasian Mountain Peoples.

But the Tatars share Kiev's hostility toward Russian policy and designs on the Crimea, a hostility thus directed against Russians. The Tatars, for example, condemned the July 1993 Russian parliamentary claim over Sevastopol, adding their support for Ukrainian territorial integrity and Ukrainian sovereignty over the Crimea.

The election of President Kuchma may reduce tension with the Crimea in the short term. More than 80 percent of Crimeans voted for Kuchma in the presidential elections because they perceived him as likely to favor closer integration with the CIS and Russia, as well as being more in favor of leasing Sevastopol to the Russian Black Sea Fleet. Relations between Kuchma and the Crimea will still remain difficult, however, and any attempt at Crimean secession would still lead to a crisis of large magnitude between Ukraine and Russia. Kuchma and the newly elected parliament have continued to strongly back tough measures against the Crimea.

Regionalism

The Ruthenian movement in Transcarpathia established a Transcarpathian Republican Party in March 1992 to press for the region's reunification with Czechoslovakia and Kiev's recognition of Ruthenians as a separate ethnic group distinct from Ukrainians. A "provisional" Transcarpathian Ruthenian government, complaining of "Ukrainian national chauvinist circles," was formed in May 1993 in Slovakia and has demanded a referendum on the oblast's status. It has expressed its desire to be "independent" and its intention to apply for separate membership in the CIS.

But the demands for greater autonomy in Transcarpathia, as in Odesa, are more economically grounded than political or secessionist. In the 1994 parliamentary elections, supporters of the Ruthenian or "New Russia" movements in Transcarpathia and Odesa failed to garner popularity in these respective regions. The danger to Ukraine's territorial integrity from these two areas is far less than that imagined in Kiev and therefore more a product of the exaggerated threat perceptions discussed in chapter 1.

Romanian groups in Chernivtsi oblast (formerly northern Bukovina) are vocal in their agitation for the return of the region to Romania. The Transcarpathian and Bukovinian questions will only become acute in the event of Ukrainian disintegration, where foreign powers may be tempted to intervene and annex adjacent border areas.

Domestic Threats

Economic

Internal threats to Ukrainian security have been regarded traditionally as less important than recognized external threats by the Ukrainian leadership, such as those associated with Russia. There was little appreciation within the former Ukrainian leadership of the importance of economic security to Ukrainian independence. As a result, Ukraine possessed no overall economic strategy and little understanding of the new wider definitions of national security discussed in the West.[36]

Economic security is damaged by hyperinflation, a declining growth rate, a large budgetary deficit (which leads to high interest rates and undermines long-term investment), corruption, and organized crime. Poor economic performance also leads to unfulfilled expectations and prevents the transfer of allegiances within the population to the newly independent state. The weaker the economy, the greater the likelihood of economic pressure, foreign influence, dependence on imports, and an inability to pay for budgetary outlays on defense.

With its relatively good transportation system, highly fertile agricultural land, and variety of mineral resources (coal, gas, oil, uranium, manganese, etc.), Ukraine could be a potential economic power. The republic produced 46 percent of the agricultural output of the former USSR. Ukraine's potential in industry, agriculture, mineral resources, and business, combined with its level of education, infrastructure, proximity to Europe, and homogeneity of population, gave it a higher rating than any other former Soviet republic.[37] But Ukraine's economic disadvantages may outweigh its advantages, given its abundance of unskilled labor, low labor productivity, high degree of unionization, lack of modern equipment, and the likelihood of a reoccurring energy shortage.[38] The legacy of the USSR has also left Ukraine with human and physical capital that requires a long-term program of restructuring—high job security, low prices, lax work ethic, high social benefits, bureaucracy, lack of responsibility and initiative, backward technology, the lack of a banking/financial sector, and inexperience in foreign trade.

Former premier Vitold Fokin's "shock without the therapy" during 1990–1992 occurred amid predictions even *before* economic reform had been implemented of the likelihood of a fall in living standards. Despite his acute mishandling of the economy, legacy of hyperinflation, and lack of reform program, Kravchuk defended Fokin as long as possible. The issuing of unbacked credit to keep enterprises and collective farms afloat in 1991–1992 reached an astronomical 491 billion *karbovantsi* (compared with only 10.4 billion in 1991).

The real reasons for the lack of personnel changes within the government in 1992 were connected to the lack of domestic pressure for economic reform and clannish ties of the national communists. Undoubtedly, Kravchuk and Fokin went back a long way and were cut from the same cloth. Also, Kravchuk, fearful of domestic strife and internal sabotage by members of the *ancien* regime (such as the creation of a separatist "Dniester Republic" in eastern Ukraine) wanted to win *and* buy over those interests that were deeply entrenched in the republic and whose power Kravchuk feared. In contrast, the Moldovan leadership, freed of domestic opposition to reform because its eastern industrial region was beyond its control, has been praised by the International Monetary Fund (IMF) and World Bank for its boldness in economic policy.

Premier Kuchma, Fokin's replacement, was formerly director of the Southern Machine Construction Plant *Pivdenmash* in eastern Ukraine (which built, among other items, SS-18 and SS-24 nuclear missiles). Kuchma's special powers to rule the economy by decree ended in mid-May 1993; finally, Kuchma resigned for the third time in September 1993.

The Kuchma government failed to implement structural reforms, its decrees failed to break the vested interests of the industrial or banking sectors, and under its leadership hyperinflation actually increased. The government was plagued by a lack of consensus on reform and by autumn 1993 was completely dominated by representatives of the "Red Directors." The departure of Viktor Penzennyk in August 1993, the last proponent of economic reform within the government, strengthened the hand of those calling for full Economic Union with Russia under threat of secession of the Donbas and Crimea from Ukraine.

The June 1993 strikes by 400,000 miners and industrial workers, primarily in eastern Ukraine, was the first indication that the domestic stability Ukraine had enjoyed until then had ended. The very people whom Kravchuk had kept in power in eastern Ukraine to maintain "stability," members of the former *ancien* regime, had deserted him and helped organize the strikes. They had also added political demands, such as autonomy and referendum on faith in president and parliament, to the economic demands of the strikers. Not only had Kravchuk lost his support in eastern Ukraine (as seen most strikingly in the June–July 1994 presidential elections), but the strikers and local leadership had rightly questioned both his lack of leadership skills and his inability to manage the economy. Eastern Ukraine was, in effect, now trying to drag the remainder of the country back into economic union with Russia.

The negative effects of the mishandling of the economy, the lack of reform upon social stability, and the difficulty of transferring the loyalties of the population to the newly independent state are painfully obvious. One of the major reasons for the growth in apathy and disillusionment in Ukraine was the feeling that in reality "nothing had changed" after December 1991: the "same people" are running the place as before. Thus, in one opinion poll, 53 percent believed that former communist structures, the old bureaucracy and *nomenklatura*, were to blame for placing a brake on reform and Ukraine's development. Only 9.52 percent blamed pressure by other republics of the former USSR.[39]

The growing economic crisis, as well as the lack of reform and economic program, was leading Ukraine toward potential disaster. This situation not only increased disillusionment with independence among the population but is allowing Russia to exert pressure because of Ukraine's domestic weakness (as reflected in the September 1993 Massandra summit).

The increasing economic crisis revealed the utter bankruptcy of the gradual approach to reform; it was the major mistake of the Kravchuk leadership, which ultimately led to Kravchuk's downfall in summer 1994. The government, dominated as it was by antireform "Red Directors," looked for salvation not to reducing hyperinflation and implementing reform–but to economic reintegration with Russia. But the economic reintegration of Russia with republics such as Ukraine and Belarus will only serve to water down the reform process in Russia itself.[40]

In October 1993 Yukhym Zviayahilskyy, former coal mine director in Donets'k and reportedly an organizer of the June 1993 miners' strikes, took over as acting premier. The government was dominated by representatives from the Donbas, people associated with the Party of Labour and UIEU (the so-called Red Directors). It is they who were directing Ukraine's cautious, slow road to market economic reform, which was close to Kravchuk's way of thinking. They were brought into government by Kravchuk to appease the Donbas and thereby ensure Ukraine's territorial integrity.

Taking over from former premier Kuchma they found Ukraine in an even worse economic crisis than that inherited from Premier Fokin in October 1992. National income had decreased by 15 percent in 1993 with hyperinflation reaching 200 percent in December (9,000 percent throughout the year). Industrial production decreased by 7.4 percent between 1993 and the previous year.[41] To escape from this crisis the new Cabinet of Ministers at times continued to talk in doublespeak: "The plan should regulate and direct economic reforms into a single groove of consistent market transformations which would ensure state control of the economy on the part of the state."[42]

No government plan could escape from the fact that Ukraine's economic crisis placed it in worse shape than any other former Soviet republic—other than war torn Georgia and Armenia. The slow pace of reforms, energy-hungry factories, inflationary credit emissions and a negative trade balance with energy suppliers Russia and Turkmenistan are some of the many symptoms afflicting the Ukrainian economy. A third of Ukraine's factories are temporarily closed while the remainder are months behind in paying their staff.[43]

The atmosphere did begin to change in the new year. On the eve of Ukrainian parliamentary elections, during the first quarter of 1994, a successful visit by an economic delegation to the United States, launch of an ambitious (for Ukraine) reform program and anti-inflationary measures, coupled with an increase in U.S. and West European aid after Ukraine's ratification of the Strategic Arms Reduction Treaty or START I, all made a difference.

In October 1994, President Kuchma unfolded a radical economic reform program that won the backing of the Ukrainian parliament and all of the country's political groups, except for the communists. For the first time in independent Ukraine's short history, a consensus has been reached throughout Ukraine over the need to implement its first serious economic reform program. The program won financial backing from the IMF, the World Bank, and the European Union (EU). In 1995 Ukraine is set to embark on economic reform at the same time that it is being reduced in Russia.

Organized Crime and Corruption

In Ukraine organized crime and corruption present one of the greatest dangers to national security because they have penetrated, and intermingled with, the state apparatus at all levels; indeed Ukraine's experience has recently been described as "hypercorruption." Former premier Kuchma told the Italian newspaper *La Respublica* that the Ukrainian mafia was even more powerful than the Sicilian.

Of the 30 million tons of oil delivered to Ukraine in 1992,

8 million tons were smuggled abroad and resold for a profit by corrupt officials. In 1992 Ukraine earned $2 billion in exports, but only $150 million were received back by the Treasury. The counterfeiting of more than 200 million Ukrainian *karbovantsi* in Poland and other republics of the former USSR, especially during the first half of 1992 when the new *karbovantsi* had no serial numbers or watermarks, severely damaged the economy and banking system, as well as fueled inflation.[44]

Ukrainian citizens reportedly hold $7 billion to $8 billion in Swiss bank accounts. In the first half of 1993, export licenses should have returned to the Ukrainian budget $4 billion, but only $100 million actually returned. The remainder is hidden in Western banks.[45]

Organized crime in Ukraine has also forged strong links with international crime and was attempting to gain control of the import-export system (narcotics, weapons, and nuclear materials), as well as diversifying into privatization and banking. In late 1992 top officials in the Ministry for Foreign Economic Relations were arrested for bribe taking and issuing of licenses to export "strategic" raw materials. Meanwhile, only a third of Western aid sent by charities and registered by Ukrainian customs actually reaches its recipients, the Red Cross, or state authorities; the remainder is swallowed up by the mafia and corruption.

At a meeting of top law enforcement officials as early as April 1992, Marchuk, the former head of the Security Service of Ukraine, admitted that regions and entire branches of the economy were falling under the sway of the mafia, who had created "support groups" in the higher echelons of authority. These fears were echoed within the population, nearly 50 percent of whom believe that Ukraine's political and economic development was being run by the mafia (with the president and parliament trailing behind).[46] Former premier Zviahilskyi is now in hiding abroad after accusations that he pocketed a minimum of $25 million while in office.

Energy Supplies and Nuclear Power

The importance of energy supplies to national security has been consistently recognized since the 1973 oil shock and 1990 Gulf

War. Overdependence upon imported energy supplies increases a country's trade deficit and produces a feeling of insecurity. This, in turn, is likely to increase demands for the greater use of nuclear power and alternative energy sources. Yet, Ukraine only imports half of its energy requirements (unlike nearly 100 percent in the Baltic republics), and its inability to pay world prices is more a reflection of economic mismanagement and failure to reorient export trade away from Russia.

Ukrainian overdependence on Russian energy supplies is a major factor preventing Ukraine from seceding from the CIS; this dependence upon Russia has traditionally been regarded as a threat to its national security. One of the many areas of dispute between Russia and Ukraine surrounds energy supplies to, and through, Ukraine. Russia has used energy supplies as a major lever in its security policy toward Ukraine. At the same time, 90 percent of Russian gas is exported to western and central Europe through Ukraine, which has given Ukraine leverage in its dealings with Russia and Turkmenistan.

Ukraine has attempted to circumvent the energy shortage and dependence upon Russian oil and gas by launching a highly ambitious program to create a tanker fleet of 40 ships with German backing and build larger oil refineries.[47] The Iranians are interested because Ukraine could become an outlet into Europe for their oil and gas, which will also be linked to newly proposed Turkmen pipelines going to western Europe through Iran and Ukraine.[48]

The Ukrainian authorities allocated nearly $2 million to build the pipeline from Iran through Azerbaijan.[49] By 1996 the three-stream pipeline is planned to supply 50 million tons of oil annually from Iran to Ukraine, representing the bulk of Ukraine's needs and removing Ukrainian dependence on Russia in this area. Iran is also to supply the bulk of Ukrainian gas needs.

In early April 1993, a Ukrainian government delegation also visited Oman, Qatar, Saudi Arabia, the United Arab Emirates, and Kuwait, where cooperation agreements were signed on matters including the supply of oil.[50] Problems remain, however, least of all Ukraine's ability to pay world prices for oil and gas. The Iranian oil pipeline is unlikely to be implemented in the face of conflict in the Transcaucasus, while the Turkish authorities have banned the passage of oil tankers through the Black Sea for ecological reasons. Ukrainian options are therefore limited, as it does not possess the hard currency to purchase energy supplies from other sources (in contrast to the availability of credits and barter with Russia).

The problem of ensuring adequate supplies of oil and gas have perceptibly altered the deep hostility previously held toward nuclear power in the aftermath of the Chornobyl nuclear accident in April 1986. Ukraine possesses 14 reactors located within 5 nuclear power plants, accounting for a third of its energy consumption. The Ukrainian National Security Council decreed in November 1992 that there was no alternative to increasing reliance upon nuclear power, and parliamentary committees have demanded the lifting of the moratorium on the building of new nuclear power stations, arguing that the future belongs to nuclear power.[51] In April 1993 parliamentary and government officials decided to put energy independence and supplies before fears of another nuclear accident and decreed that the moratorium on continuing the Chornobyl nuclear plant after its 1993 deadline should be dropped.

Two problems, however, concern the newfound interest in nuclear power in Ukraine. First, although uranium is mined in Ukraine, it cannot undergo a full production cycle, as no plants are capable of enriching uranium or disposing of the waste. This would mean reliance upon Russia or searching for alternative supplies, as with oil and gas. There are even indications that Ukraine's nuclear power plants could run out of fuel if payments are not made to Russia.

Second, the safety standards of Ukraine's nuclear plants leave a lot to be desired. Any accidents could again threaten whole swaths of territory throughout Europe and lead to large casualties in Ukraine and its neighbors, as in April 1986. In 1992, automatic safety systems at one nuclear power station near Odesa were switched off three times to boost production, a policy similar to the one that led to the Chornobyl nuclear accident. Ukrainian nuclear reactors were shut down on seven occasions in 1992, five of which were due to equipment failures, and a fire occurred in the nuclear power plant at Zaporizhzhia in May 1993. Ukraine's growing reliance upon nuclear power will be perceived as a potential environmental threat by its neighbors. In April 1995 Ukraine agreed, under Western pressure, to close Chornobyl by the year 2000.

Again, the role of Western aid will be crucial in dealing with Ukraine's energy problems. The G-7 nations, the United States, and the EU countries have all expressed interest in aiding Ukraine's nuclear energy program, which Ukraine has been forced to increasingly rely upon. Ukraine is also likely to depend less upon Russian energy supplies when economic reform restructures and closes unprofitable state industries traditionally reliant on cheap Russian oil and gas.

Conclusion

Although the newly independent Ukrainian state faces a number of security threats, the leadership and majority of political groups have tended to overconcentrate on, and partly exaggerate, external threats almost to the exclusion of others. Poor relations with Russia have contributed to this situation, resulting in Ukraine's neglect of domestic reform. There was a continued failure to recognize the economic dimensions of its security problems.[52] The desire to hang onto independence at any cost, given a record of previous failures, has blinded many nationalist groups to the growing internal threats to Ukrainian independence, which are likely to prove the decisive factor in Ukrainian security.

Former president Kravchuk may have successfully won over the *ancien* regime to independence in the short term, thereby preventing ethnic instability, but it was paid for with a heavy price and missed opportunities. Corruption, stagnation, and entrenchment of the old ruling class prevented progress in political and economic reform, as well as leading to widespread disillusionment within the population and growing discontent among national minorities. Certainly, "hypercorruption" and organized crime will have to be challenged in a more serious manner than hitherto has been the case, especially as it has penetrated all levels of the state apparatus, a factor recognized by newly elected president Kuchma. Corruption is a reinforcing factor in the wide-spread public nihilism toward the legitimacy of the newly independent state.

The disintegration of the center ground that Kravchuk represents was a product of the breakdown of national consensus and deep political and economic crisis. During 1992–1994, Kravchuk lost his popular base in western and eastern Ukraine for patriotic, political, and economic reasons. Only during the presidential elections in June 1994 did western-central Ukraine rally to Kravchuk because of its hostility toward the other main "pro-Russian" contender (Kuchma). Reorienting Ukrainian citizens, especially the large Russian minority, is proving difficult, as is establishing the legitimacy of the independent state. The growth of pro-Russian and regionalist sentiments may increase, thereby reducing national consensus and stability even further, which has certainly placed federalization and closer CIS integration on the Ukrainian political agenda. Nationalist demands for secession from the CIS are only supported by a minority of the population, which believes that it could lead to ethnic strife and deeper economic crisis.

The low Ukrainian priority given to economic reform can be attributed to the lack of domestic pressure in support of it (both nationalists and national communists gave it low priority while there was a lack of competent staff to implement it), coupled with a lack of conviction and direction for it at the presidential level. Only the New Ukraine bloc and Inter-Regional Bloc of Reforms consistently argued for political and economic reform and a more sober assessment of Ukraine's need for economic cooperation within the CIS. But New Ukraine is unpopular in Western Ukraine, where support for economic reform is highest. Nevertheless, President Kuchma has been successful in forging for the first time an all-Ukrainian majority consensus on reform, and his popularity ratings remained high at 60–70 percent during his first year in office.

The growing political and economic crisis is already undermining Ukrainian independence. The previous lack of any economic reform program, a conservative and incompetent parliament coupled with a president lacking in vision and leadership proved catastrophic for Ukrainian independence. The growing domestic crisis prevented the formation of a national consensus in Ukraine with regard to its national interests and the appropriate degree to which relations should be enhanced or downgraded with its neighbors. This, in turn, reflected the continuing and growing internal divisions over the priority which should be given to different security policies, in particular a pro, anti or neutral Russian orientation.

If Ukraine fails to address the political and economic crisis, the threat of disintegration is likely to grow, as reflected in the deep divisions brought out by the elections held in 1994. This situation has at last been recognized by President Kuchma. It is the main threat to Ukrainian security; without a solution to these questions, separatism and regionalism will grow. The improvement of relations with Russia is also a *quid pro quo* to prevent excessive concentration upon security questions while neglecting domestic reform. These are two areas where President Kuchma has prioritized his administration. Ukrainian independence is threatened by either a nationalistic backlash, which will inflame relations with Russia and alienate regions and national minorities, or a forced reintegration with Russia, which will not be accepted by a large proportion of the Ukrainian population, leadership, and armed forces. A balance between these two extremes is vital for Ukrainian security; this should be a policy priority for newly elected Ukrainian leaders as well as Western policymakers.

3

Foreign Policy and
International Relations

Ukrainian foreign policy did not start from zero in December 1991. Kiev had a small but professional diplomatic staff that had worked in UN agencies since the United Nations was founded in 1945. In addition, Ukrainian diplomatic activity, which was launched immediately after the July 1990 Declaration of Sovereignty, has always been supported by a large and vocal Ukrainian emigré lobby in North America. Emigré funding and the provision of property, for example, have been largely instrumental in ensuring the establishment of Ukraine's large diplomatic presence in Western countries, an important plank of Ukrainian foreign policy during the first year of independence.

Ukrainian foreign policy during 1992 concentrated on a number of areas. First, official visits by former president Kravchuk, former parliamentary chairman Ivan Pliushch, and former foreign minister Anatoliy Zlenko were undertaken frequently and to a large variety of countries that were strategically important in Kiev's eyes.

Second, only Ukraine and the three Baltic republics (Russia inherited former Soviet premises) pursued a policy of establishing diplomatic presence on the ground in these strategically important countries. In both cases, Kiev believed that becoming a factor on the international stage and in Western capitals contributed to strengthening Ukraine's security by ensuring that an independent Ukrainian state was an established and visible actor.

The intellectual foundation for Ukrainian foreign policy

came only a year later. In mid-1993, the Ukrainian parliament adopted the Basic Principles of Ukrainian foreign policy, which included some reference to Ukraine's national interests. This was followed by a military doctrine in the autumn. But the outgoing parliament failed to adopt a national security policy. Ukrainian foreign and military policy did not crystallize until the summer and autumn of 1993, one additional factor that dragged out the process of Ukraine's ratification of START I, much to the annoyance of the West. It is no coincidence that the Ukrainian parliament ratified START I less than a month after it ratified its military doctrine, which shaped Kiev's attitudes to the nuclear weapons on its territory.

Throughout this period, a central factor of Ukrainian foreign policy has remained a search for security to buttress the military capabilities of the newly independent state. This has included becoming a member of Western institutions, where possible, or joining the queue for membership in other cases. Although remaining hostile to the CIS collective security treaty, Ukraine was the first CIS member to join NATO's "Partnership for Peace" program. Second, Ukraine proposed a number of security initiatives itself in Central Europe and the Black Sea region. Third, Ukraine has developed a close dialogue and cooperation with countries that have similar threats to their territorial integrity (China, India, Turkey, Moldova, and others).

This chapter outlines the main directions of Ukrainian foreign and security policy during the first three years of independence and then surveys Ukraine's relations with the West, CIS/Russia, Central Europe, and key Middle Eastern and Asian countries. Finally, it discusses the key elements of Ukrainian foreign policy and its likely future direction.

Evolution of Ukrainian Foreign Policy

Upon independence, Ukraine inherited a small diplomatic staff, particularly from UN agencies in New York, Paris, Geneva, and Vienna. Former foreign minister Zlenko previously was employed in UNESCO in Paris.[1] Ukrainian diplomats worked from

Soviet embassies in the United States, Canada, and Germany. The Croatian president told his Ukrainian hosts that he envied them because their UN membership had given them a head start.[2]

But for a country of Ukraine's size, the staff was small and inadequate. In January 1992 the staff of the Ukrainian Ministry of Foreign Affairs numbered fewer than 400. The Ukrainian media devoted sparse attention to foreign affairs, which created a high degree of provincialism and overconcentration on domestic issues, such as state building. Concepts such as the dangers of nuclear proliferation were absent from the Ukrainian nuclear debate; the subject was both distant and irrelevant for the domestic audience.

In contrast to Ukraine, Russia inherited the diplomatic, journalistic, and specialist staff of the former USSR with their acute, professional knowledge of foreign affairs and the workings of international relations. Hence it was far easier for Russia to reformulate its national interests, role, and place in international relations vis-à-vis the former USSR.

A major policy of Ukraine during 1992 was simply to increase Ukraine's presence on the international stage by establishing embassies and consulates and making official visits.[3] Ukraine established an international airline with leased Western aircraft and direct routes to Kiev, issuing visas at all entry points into the country from March 1992. Ukrainian foreign policy, according to Zlenko, aimed to put Ukraine on the global map as an independent entity and a subject of international law.

In spring 1992, Ukraine's foreign policy in the intermediate period, when statehood was being consolidated, was geared toward five main areas: Ukraine's neighbors, especially the Visegrad Group and increasingly Russia and the CIS; countries with large Ukrainian minorities (the United States and Canada); the territorial units of larger countries, such as Bavaria; the West; and finally, special interest countries, such as the Vatican and Israel.[4]

By the end of 1992, the lack of more clear-cut guidelines for Ukrainian foreign policy began to come under scrutiny. "The president of Ukraine is traveling around, but the voice of a great European country is not heard. The concept of a foreign policy is not apparent," commented one newspaper.[5] The criticism was largely misguided. Ukraine wanted to establish an immediate presence on the international stage to secure its independence in the world's eyes, prior to the intellectual elaboration of its national security policy and national interests.

Nevertheless, numerous geopolitical questions remained outstanding. They included joining the Visegrad group, building relations with Western Europe, engaging in conflict management in Moldova (and later the Transcaucasus), building an alliance with Belarus, and playing a role in the Yugoslav conflict where 100,000 Ukrainians had lived (the Ukrainian center of Banja Luka is now the Bosnian Serbs' main base). Ukraine could have used these issues, particularly Moldova and Yugoslavia, to play an international role, "as an independent partner and not as a state on Russia's outskirts."[6] The Ukrainian leadership also missed the opportunity during 1992 to go the Baltic way and reorient the country away from Russia and the CIS toward the West. It must be added, however, that Ukraine, in contrast to the Baltic states, was not a welcome new member of the international community of nations during this period.

The majority of these geopolitical issues were ducked, particularly where Russian intervention was taking place in Moldova and the Transcaucasus. Yet, turning a blind eye to Russian imperialism in the hope that Ukraine would not be targeted at a later date has proved to be folly. By 1994, with the bulk of the former USSR back under Moscow's wings, Ukraine was firmly in Russia's sights.

On July 5, 1993, the Ukrainian parliament adopted the "Basic Principles of Ukraine's Foreign Policy," which would determine the direction of Ukraine's geopolitical strategy.[7] The principles are divided into four main areas—Ukraine's national interests and foreign policy objectives; foreign policy principles; the direction, priorities and functions of foreign policy; and the mechanics of pursuing this policy. They are still the guidelines for the new Ukrainian leadership elected in 1994.

Ukraine's national interests were formulated as the strategic and geopolitical interests relating to national security and independence, economic interests (including integration within the world economy), and regional and local interests. Ukrainian foreign policy rejected any single state as the sole successor to the former USSR, condemned the presence of foreign troops on the territories of former Soviet non-Russian republics, and opposed Russian demands for UN/Conference on Security and Cooperation in Europe (CSCE) mandates for peacekeeping.

The foreign policy principles aimed to develop Ukraine's relations in four directions. These included international relations, broad European regional cooperation, CIS cooperation, and membership of international organizations. These foreign policy directions would be undertaken with the help of joining security systems, such as the CSCE, by enlarging their responsibilities.

Mykola Mikhailchenko, former president Kravchuk's influential political adviser, pointed to the only three options available, given that the bulk of the world community did not want to see an economically and politically powerful Ukraine. These were Eurocentric (entering Europe through regional alliances), Eurasiatic (in alliance with Russia and the CIS), and neutral.[8]

During 1992–1993, Ukraine maintained a policy of neutrality primarily as a means to reject Russian pressure to join the CIS Collective Security Agreement. As a result, Ukraine has not officially applied for NATO or WEU membership, although it is a member of the North Atlantic Cooperation Council (NACC) and NATO's "Partnership for Peace." Zlenko explained the dichotomy: "Our geopolitical position does not permit Ukraine to be neutral in the classic sense of the word. . . ." The Polish foreign minister rejected this neutrality; if Kiev wanted to join such Western structures as the EU and was already a member of NACC, then it could not be "neutral," he claimed.[9] Despite its positive record on national minority rights, Ukraine has still not been admitted to the Council of Europe because it has not yet adopted a new (post-Soviet) constitution. These steps are likely to be taken in the second half of 1995.

Ukraine repeatedly expressed an interest in joining the Visegrad group as a stepping-stone to the creation of a Central European Security Zone (see below) and other regional organizations. This is tied to Ukraine's attempts to join security structures independent of the CIS. Speaking at the UN, Zlenko called upon the CSCE to become a new forum to shape European security. Ukraine's national security would be best served by its membership in a "future all-European system of collective security." Ukraine has argued in favor of the creation of CSCE peacekeeping forces based on NATO and the WEU to ensure security throughout Europe (including the CIS).[10]

Ukraine was the first CIS member to join NATO's "Partnership for Peace" program on February 8, 1994, calling it a "reasonable and pragmatic alternative to partial and selective NATO enlargement." Ukraine has been cautious about the incorporation of new NATO members, feeling that it would isolate Ukraine in the face of Russian pressure by building a new "Berlin Wall" on its Western borders. Former Ukrainian ambassador to Belgium Volodymyr Vasylenko explained that Ukraine was against a partial expansion of NATO because "this would leave Ukraine in a grey zone between an enlarged NATO and Russia."[11] Yet NATO had established the program without consulting Ukraine, despite the fact that geographically Ukraine – not Russia – bordered Central Europe (except in Kalingrad).

Anton Buteiko, former presidential adviser on foreign affairs, stated that the program would "strengthen our international prestige and give us additional security guarantees."[12] The assistant to the NATO secretary general for political issues, Gerhardt von Moltke, told his Ukrainian audience in Kiev that the NATO program provides an opportunity to conduct joint operations with NATO in the event of a threat to Ukrainian territorial integrity.[13] Ukraine would be an active member of the program and bring its armed forces up to standards in order to be eligible for future NATO membership. Former president Kravchuk called the initiative "an important step . . . in building a European security system, in bringing together Eastern and Western Europe."[14]

The election of President Kuchma and the large left-wing bloc in the new Ukrainian parliament have a clear pro-Russian/CIS orientation; hence the Communist Party instructed its supporters to vote for Kuchma in the second round of the presidential elections. Kuchma may expand Ukraine's membership in the CIS Economic Union as a full member although he has rejected rejoining the ruble zone (which may even become unpopular in Russia, given its difficulty in financing the Belarusian monetary union).

But the paths of these two groups are as likely to conflict as they are to converge. Indeed, President Kuchma has no choice but to confront the communist lobby in parliament in his promotion of economic reform in a manner akin to President Yeltsin. In addition, President Kuchma is acutely aware that he has a slim mandate of only 7 percent, which will not allow major geopolitical changes to Ukraine's strategic orientation without leading to acute domestic instability and fierce domestic nationalist opposition. He has thus rejected political-military integration in the CIS and avoided his predecessor's description of Ukraine as a "buffer" between Europe and Russia, instead referring to Ukraine as a "bridge."

The United States and the West[15]

During 1992–1993, U.S. policy toward Ukraine was monopolized by the question of nuclear weapons and an exclusive focus upon Russia. Ukraine's failure to ratify START I and the Lisbon Protocol as well as the Nuclear Nonproliferation Treaty (NPT), despite Kravchuk's repeated promises to do so, was a major, but not the only, reason for deteriorating U.S.-Ukrainian relations and Kiev's disillusionment with the West.

Without taking into account the deeply entrenched insecurity complex of the Ukrainian leadership vis-à-vis Russia, U.S. policy was destined to fail in 1992–1993. Kiev consistently complained that its size and strategic importance were ignored by the United States, thereby giving it only nuclear weapons to obtain Western attention, that the United States continued to look at Ukraine through "Russian eyes" with Ukraine regarded as merely an appendage of Russia.

Former president George Bush's Russocentric policies undoubtedly contributed to the growth of the pronuclear lobby and even anti-Americanism in Ukraine.[16] These views within the former Ukrainian parliament influenced the desire to hold onto nuclear weapons and were succinctly spelled out by former premier, now president, Kuchma: "The real problem is that the West is indifferent to whether we are independent."[17] Until such attitudes were taken into account by Western policymakers, they could not understand the domestic sources of the pronuclear lobby in Ukraine.

Although the impression was certainly created in Kiev that U.S. foreign policy toward Ukraine was monopolized by nuclear weapons, this was only partly the case. Certainly Russia obtained (or was promised) the lion's share of Western aid (of the $1.8 billion in aid pledged to the former USSR in Tokyo, only $300 million, or 17 percent, was for the non-Russians),[18] but Ukraine also failed to fully appreciate that a stable, reformist Russia was in its own security interests. U.S. aid to Ukraine through the Agency for International Development, IMF, and World Bank have still been substantial. In addition, there are a large number of U.S.-funded technical and humanitarian aid projects through government departments in Ukraine.

Often the problem was twofold. On the one hand, Ukraine's lack of commitment to political and economic reform, in comparison to Russia, gave it a bad image, together with the West's wrongly held perception of Ukraine as the "spoiler republic" within the CIS. On the other hand, U.S. aid to the non-Russian republics, including Ukraine, was often an afterthought and labeled misleadingly as "Russian aid" or aid to the "Newly Independent States." While Western Europeans demanded the right to defend their national sovereignty against the Maastricht Treaty, Ukraine's attempts to do likewise within the CIS were often castigated as that of the "spoiler republic."

By spring 1993, the dilemma for the United States was twofold: either develop a stronger, more broadly based relationship with Ukraine, at the risk of harming relations with Russia, or rebuff Ukrainian complaints and leave it to move toward becoming a full-fledged nuclear power with all the attendant negative consequences. A closer security relationship between the United States and Ukraine risked Russian disapproval. By early 1994 the dilemma had been solved. The end of the Russian-U.S. honeymoon gave a window of opportunity for U.S.-Ukrainian relations to improve in the aftermath of Kiev's ratification of START I.

The U.S.-Russian summit in March 1993 was perceived in Kiev as the continuation of former president Bush's Russocentric policies. But during May and June, the summit was followed by visits to Kiev by Strobe Talbott, then ambassador-at-large to the CIS, and Les Aspin, former U.S. secretary of defense. Their visits reflected the realization that previous U.S. policy had dramatically failed. Instead of talk of "pressure," the United States was now looking at "Ukraine's very legitimate requirements for maximum security" and proposing "new fresh approaches and ideas." Talbott talked of drawing up a charter of U.S.-Ukrainian bilateral relations, support for economic reform, conversion of the military industrial complex, military cooperation, and proposing U.S. services as an intermediary to resolve outstanding disputes between Ukraine and Russia. Finally, Aspin stressed that Ukraine's independence was in the "U.S. interest."

During the first quarter of 1994, U.S.-Ukrainian relations improved dramatically as a consequence of two factors. First, the Ukrainian parliament ratified START I and dropped the reservations it had attached in November 1993 (see chapter 4). Second, government circles and the media within the United States began to debate the strategic significance of independent Ukraine. These two events, in turn, occurred at the same time as the end of the Russian-U.S. honeymoon.[19] Proposals for a new U.S.-Russian "partnership" have faded, particularly in the light of Russian foreign minister Andrei Kozyrev's playing to the nationalist constituency since December 1993.[20]

The nationalist-communist victory in the December 1993 Russian elections, resignation of reformers from the Russian government,[21] Russian intervention on Serbia's side in the Bosnian conflict, the Aldrich Ames CIA scandal,[22] growing disquiet at Russian imperialism in the former USSR,[23] and fear of a post-Yeltsin Russian presidency[24] all contributed to the debate over whether Russia could any longer be trusted as an "ally" and "partner." Strobe Talbott, former ambassador-at-large to the CIS, was criticized for bringing his pro-Russia bias to his post.

The changing focus of the U.S. debate strengthened support for Ukraine within the U.S. administration. Zbigniew Brzezinski argued for U.S. policy to become "the consolidation of geopolitical pluralism within the former Soviet Union" as a "necessary precondition for the eventual emergence of a stable democratic Russia." Brzezinski condemned U.S. policy for turning a blind eye to Russian intervention in the former USSR and recreation of an empire in the form of a CIS confederation under Moscow's control. Yet, Russia can "be either an empire or a democracy, but it cannot be both." Brzezinski finally reminded his readers that Russia cannot become an empire without Ukraine. Ukrainian independence is thus the key to the future of Russian democracy.[25]

On his return from a visit to Russia and Ukraine, former president Richard Nixon also argued that "the independence of Ukraine is indispensable. . . . Ukrainian stability is in the strategic interests of the United States." Any Russian aggression against or destabilization of Ukraine would have "devastating consequences" for U.S.-Russian relations. Nixon told former national security officials that the United States must adopt a "hard line" on protecting Ukrainian independence, making clear in advance that it would "fight to prevent a Russian takeover."[26]

Nevertheless, not all U.S. and Western policies of appeasement of Russia were immediately dropped. According to Russian presidential adviser Andranik Migranian, "the U.S. side has confirmed Russia's special role in maintaining stability in the post-Soviet space" at the January 1994 Moscow summit. Secretary of State Warren Christopher has repeatedly excused hard-line statements by the Russian leadership, claiming they were only for domestic audiences. Christopher "detected good signs" in the Russian military doctrine and President Yeltsin's State of the Union address.[27] Appeasement of hard-line Russian sentiments such as these only serve to sharpen Ukrainian insecurity and increase distrust of U.S. intentions and commitments to its obligations—for example, security assurances on Ukrainian territorial integrity.

Former president Kravchuk's visit to the United States in early March 1994 cemented the new U.S.-Ukrainian relationship further.[28] U.S. aid to Ukraine was doubled to $700 million, half as economic aid and the remainder for nuclear disarmament. The economic aid is conditional, "upon appropriate steps to implement concrete economic reforms necessary for assistance to be effective." International financial institutions were putting together a plan to support Ukrainian economic reforms with credits of $3.5 billion over two years. This was followed by a partnership and cooperation agreement with the EU that covers political dialogue, improved trade, and investment opportunities. Ukraine is to join the EU free trade zone in 1998 and hopes to eventually join the EU as a full member.[29] The EU has also offered aid to deal with Ukraine's energy problems by reducing its dependence on nuclear power.

President Clinton also "strongly reaffirmed American support for Ukraine's independence, sovereignty and territorial integrity" during Kravchuk's visit. Kravchuk used the growing distrust of the United States toward Russian policies as a way of promoting Ukraine as a buffer.

Relations between the West and Ukraine improved dramatically under President Kuchma in the second half of 1994. The two issues that had held back any improvement – nuclear disarmament and economic reform – were addressed. President Kuchma introduced an all-embracing, radical economic and political reform program that was backed by parliament. It obtained nationwide consensus and was endorsed by international financial institutions that agreed to provide monetary aid. In October-November 1994, Kuchma paid two highly successful visits to the United States and Canada that produced further pledges of financial aid and political support to Ukraine from the G-7. At the December CSCE summit in Budapest, when the CSCE became known as the Organization for Security and Cooperation in Europe (OSCE), the Ukrainian parliament's ratification of the NPT was rewarded with the signing of a memorandum of security assurances by the five nuclear powers. Continuing deterioration of relations between the West and Russia during the Chechnya crisis is likely to lead the West to further upgrade its relations with Ukraine.

Within Western Europe, Ukraine's number one partner is Germany although Ukraine's relations with Germany have not progressed as fast as Kiev would have preferred. A major reason for this is that Poland and Russia are always likely to be Germany's priorities in central-eastern Europe. Russophilism and nostalgia for Russia remains powerful within the ranks of the German elite, which, as late as February 1993, had not a single German expert on Ukrainian affairs.[30] During 1992-1993, Ukraine thus figured as a low priority in German foreign policy, except in Bavaria, which has close religious and historical ties with western Ukraine. Perhaps Bonn also felt constrained by the continued presence (until August 1994) of Russian troops on the territory of the former German Democratic Republic.

After the disintegration of the former USSR, relations belatedly improved, especially on the economic front where Germany soon became the largest foreign investor in Ukraine. Of all humanitarian aid supplied to Ukraine, the largest amount (56.4 percent) was provided by Germany (in contrast to 4.3 percent by the United States).[31] By early 1994 the greatest amount of West European aid to Ukraine was provided by Germany (DM30 million), while 120 German joint ventures operated in Ukraine.

Germany's relations with Ukraine only became relatively important in early 1994. Ukrainian ratification of START I removed the threat of a nuclear Ukraine, which many had argued would inevitably lead to a nuclear Germany. Repeating U.S. concerns, German chancellor Helmut Kohl told Russia it should respect the territorial integrity of neighboring states and build trust among them, rather than creating spheres of influence. These views were echoed by British defense minister Malcolm Rifkind, who warned that imperialistic statements were now also originating in the democratic camp.[32]

Former Ukrainian foreign minister Zlenko visited Germany in February 1994, where his counterpart, Klaus Kinkel, promised continued economic aid and integration within European security structures. In return, Kiev agreed to support Germany's efforts to join an enlarged UN Security Council.[33] Next Ukrainian defense minister Radetskyi visited Germany, where a declaration was signed detailing cooperation in the restructuring of armed forces, training, and arms control. The dialogue over security policy, launched in Kiev in August 1993 by German defense minister Volker Ruehe, would continue through Ukraine's membership in NATO's "Partnership for Peace" and the partnership and cooperation agreement with the EU.[34]

The CIS and Russia

During 1993-1994 Russia successfully transformed the CIS into a confederation, despite Ukrainian objections. It is now evolving in the direction of a new Eurasian Union of the former Soviet states. These trends will continue and undoubtedly bring it into conflict with Ukraine after 1995-1996, when Russia holds fresh presidential and parliamentary elections.

The development of a two-tier CIS was probably inevitable in view of the widely differing definitions of its role. Ukraine was always more keen to endorse socioeconomic rather than military-political agreements. Therefore, it was natural that Russia would move closer to Belarus and Central Asia, both of whom had always favored closer integration. As the CIS stagnated or stood still, bilateral relations took over, a development favored by those countries who opposed its transformation into a confederation.

The first idea of an Economic Union was put forward by Gorbachev, with strong Western backing, as a stepping-stone to the new Union Treaty. Ukraine rejected the original draft proposed in October 1991 because the amendments it demanded had not been made, and it opposed the link between an economic and political union made by Soviet and Russian leaders. Those republics that today are still in favor of close integration with Russia (the Central Asian republics and Belarus) appealed to Kiev that they could not "imagine the union without Ukraine."[35] A month later Ukraine finally signed the Economic Union Treaty when some of its 25 demands were taken into consideration, but only after stormy objections by the Ukrainian parliament.

Kravchuk's newly held view that the CIS should no longer be terminated but remodeled into an EC-style structure was implemented in May 1993 at a meeting of CIS heads of state. Kravchuk signed an instruction to the premiers to prepare a document on creating an economic community that would include all CIS members. In a manner similar to the creation of the CIS, in July 1993 the three, Slavic republics—Russia, Belarus, and Ukraine—signed a draft Economic Union treaty that did not include the reservations made by both Kravchuk and then powerful chairman of the Ukrainian parliament Ivan Pliushch.[36]

The closeness of the two proposals for Economic Union (autumn 1991 and summer 1993) made it highly unpopular in Ukraine, even among moderates. Volodymyr Lanovyi, former deputy premier and a leading proponent of market economic reform, argued that the Economic Union was mainly a "political act." In the view of Chornovil, leader of Rukh, the Economic Union was an attempt to create a federation "identical to the model of the former USSR and continuation of the Novo-Ogarevo process started by Gorbachev and suspended by the August 1991 coup."

Kravchuk only agreed to join the Economic Union as an associate member. Again this was a compromise between both opposing camps (full membership and withdrawal from it). Certainly, public opinion polls testify to the regional breakdown in hostility or support for an Economic Union with Russia. Whereas Kiev and western-central Ukraine are, on the whole, hostile to the treaty, the inhabitants of eastern-southern Ukraine and the Crimea are more inclined to favor it. The Crimean leadership issued a statement that emphatically disagreed with Ukraine's becoming only an associate member. This position reflected Kiev's readiness to make concessions to those forces bent on "isolationism." If Ukraine were not to sign the Economic Union, the Sevastopol city council threatened to hold a referendum asking if Crimeans would like to join the Economic Union as a separate entity to Ukraine. The council also supported a military union with Russia and lease of Sevastopol.[37]

The Ukrainian authorities perceive their main *external* threat as deriving from Russia. Yet there is a wide gulf between Ukrainian perceptions of the real and perceived threats from Russia, which are clouded by the historical legacy of their troubled relations (as outlined in earlier chapters). Territorial claims have traditionally come from the legislative, and not executive, branch of the Russian leadership (that is, from parliament rather than president or government).

The Russian military is a "fractured, directionless, demoralised and politically disenfranchised institution." It will require a decade to rebuild it so that it could be in a position to threaten its neighbors.[38] Although the majority of the Ukrainian elite and political parties believe Russia to be a military threat, Russia's armed forces are in no condition to mount a full-scale military offensive against Ukraine in the near future. The only exception is the Black Sea Fleet, whose 48,000 officers and enlisted men are sufficient in size to fuel a Russian-Ukrainian conflict.

Russia has inherited disorganized armed forces that have lost their forward defenses and bases. These inherited divisions are at lower readiness with older military equipment, such as second echelon aircraft and tanks. Russia also lost to Ukraine shipbuilding and ship repair yards. In addition, the correlation in Ukraine's favor is 3:1 over Russia in terms of quality of equipment, weapons, and combat-ready divisions inherited by both countries in the European region of the former USSR.[39] Ukraine was home to the first strategic echelon of the former Soviet armed forces and inherited approximately 30 percent of the military equipment west of the Urals in 1991. Clearly then, there are other sources of Ukrainian insecurity than an immediate military threat.

Russians never regarded the incorporation of Ukrainian territories within their empire as anything other than their rightful claim to the inheritance of the medieval state of Kiev Rus', from which the three east Slavic nations claim their origins. A large number of Russians have therefore found it difficult to accept Ukrainian independence as a permanent phenomenon: "Millions of Russians are convinced that, without Ukraine, it is impossible to speak not only of a great Russia, but of any kind of Russia at all," the editor of *Moscow News* believes. Ukrainian independence challenges the Russian national identity as does no other republic of the former USSR.[40]

Russia and Ukraine are in dispute over many issues, including the future direction of the CIS, frontiers, Russian national minority, nuclear weapons, the Black Sea Fleet, former Soviet assets, energy supplies, and debts incurred between the Russian and Ukrainian central banks, not to mention competition for Western aid and attention.[41] The continuation of these disputes and mutual mudslinging has produced a de facto cold war between both republics since the disintegration of the former USSR. Sixty-two percent of Ukrainians thought that Ukrainian-Russian relations were either "cold" or "poor," compared with only 26 percent who believed they were "friendly" and "normal."[42] This overall level of tension is likely to subside in the aftermath of President Kuchma's victory, although initial hopes for a rapid "normalization" of relations have been disappointed.

Russian and Ukrainian national interests are also diverse and often incompatible. Ukrainians have tended to support the underdogs in the Yugoslav civil war or remain impartial, while the majority of Russians support the Serbs. In addition, in the Transcaucasus, Ukraine has similar interests to Turkey (but not Russia). Not only do Ukrainian interests include limiting Russia's sphere of influence, but Kiev supports the territorial integrity of post-Soviet states and sees a parallel between separatism within the Transcaucasian republics and the Crimea and Moldova. Ukrainian officers have trained and allegedly supplied military equipment to the Azerbaijani armed forces (including tanks and aircraft) who are fighting Armenia, a close ally of Russia in the region. Ukrainian paramilitaries have also fought with the Georgians against Abkhaz separatists allegedly supported by Russia and with separatists in Chechnya.

Of Russia's three main political blocs, only the "Westernizers," who were associated with President Yeltsin, accepted the independence of the other Soviet republics, including Ukraine. Although this support is now waning, with the bulk of the former democratic camp now supporting the revival of a new Union (whether it is called a commonwealth, confederation, or even empire is really irrelevant in Kiev's eyes). But Foreign Minister Kozyrev argued as early as summer 1992 that there could be no certainty regarding Ukrainian territorial integrity, which could be changed by peaceful means.[43] In addition, both President Yeltsin and Foreign Minister Kozyrev have gradually adopted the interventionist policies first formulated by Alexander Rutskoi's Civic Union of transforming the CIS into a confederation with Russia as the dominant state. This evolution toward a more nationalistic agenda continued, as evidenced by the Chechnya crisis in winter 1994–1995.

The center-right Civic Union united powerful moderately nationalist and industrial groups that were essentially restorationist. Although they are no longer a political force in the current Russian parliament, their center-right neoimperialist policies toward the former USSR are now the dominant policy within Russia's leading circles. The policies of the government, the foreign and defense ministries, which encounter little opposition from a weak president, support a reintegration of the former Soviet republics into a CIS confederation and close Russian ties with the "Near Abroad" (the non-Russian republics of the former USSR).

In February 1993 the growing conservative influence over Russian foreign policy was reflected in Yeltsin's proposal at a meeting of the "centrist" Civic Union that the United Nations grant Russia certain rights to maintain stability and peace within the geopolitical space of the former USSR[44] (a proposal originally put forward by a member of the Civic Union and head of the former Russian Supreme Soviet committee on foreign relations, Evgenii Ambartsumov, six months earlier).[45]

A major factor contributing to growing Ukrainian insecurity long before the December 1993 Russian elections was the vocal and persistent demand by Kozyrev for Russia to be given UN and CSCE mandates to undertake peacekeeping operations throughout the former USSR, a demand backed by the establishment of a government agency to defend the rights of Russians living outside the Russian federation. Prior to the success of Vladimir Zhirinovsky in the December 1993 elections, Russia's role as *primus inter pares* within the former USSR was favorably received by many Western governments. (Kozyrev and Douglas Hurd, UK foreign secretary, even went so far as to pen a joint article on the subject of peacekeeping.)[46]

Yet how could Western governments, unlike the Ukrainians and Balts, have misunderstood the real motives for "peacekeeping"? After all, Kozyrev has openly admitted that peacekeeping forces were particularly concerned not to "lose geopolitical positions that took centuries to conquer" in the "Near Abroad."[47]

Western policy has therefore served merely to exacerbate Ukrainian insecurity by appeasing Russian imperialism. Whenever the Russian Foreign Ministry demanded the right to undertake peacekeeping missions to "defend the 25 million Russians" outside the Russian Federation, alarm bells rang in Kiev. Nearly half of this Russian diaspora lives in Ukraine (including a million and a half in the highly sensitive Crimea). The right to intervene militarily on behalf of these Russians has been outlined in the new military doctrine, which was not criticized by Western governments.[48] Kozyrev and Russian defense minister Pavel Gaehev repeated their view that Russia had the right to militarily intervene on behalf of Russians in April 1995.

Ukrainians were particularly alarmed at the prospect of a nationalist, such as Alexander Rutskoi or Zhirinovsky, becoming Russian president after Yeltsin in 1996. For Rutskoi any separation of Ukraine and Russia is simply impossible; it would only lead to Ukraine's eventual "Lebanonization" (that is, by encouraging separatist movements, as in the Transcaucasus, and applying pressure to reintegrate the non-Russian republics under Russian influence).[49] Rutskoi has also consistently argued that "Russia's" borders cannot be confused with those of the Russian Federation while claiming that the "Crimea must never be allowed to become Ukrainian. Because from time immemorial it has been Russian Land, and it is soaked with the blood of our ancestors."[50]

The "National Patriots" include the extreme left and right in Russian politics and have close ties to the military, security services, and Ministry of Interior circles.[51] Zhirinovsky, leader of the so-called Liberal Democratic Party (LDP), came in third in the 1991 Russian presidential elections with nearly 8 percent of the vote and received the largest number of votes accorded any party in the December 1993 Russian elections. Sixty to eighty percent of the Russian military are estimated to have voted for Zhirinovsky's LDP.[52]

One of the largest national patriotic groups, the National Salvation Front, threatened military action against Ukraine if it came to power; it established branches in the Crimea with the hope of provoking conflict between Ukraine and Russia. Sergei Baburin, leader of the strongest former parliamentary faction opposed to Yeltsin, the Russian National Union, was instrumental in opening up the Crimean question, reportedly saying that "either Ukraine reunites again with Russia or there will be war."[53]

The "National Patriots" in power in Russia would provoke a full-scale Yugoslav-style civil war between Ukraine and Russia, with the ethnically mixed Donbas and Crimea playing the same role as Bosnia, sandwiched between two main protagonists. In the same manner, a nationalistic Russian president would also likely lead to the disintegration of the Russian Federation by provoking a civil war negatively affecting relations with hitherto close allies in central Asia.

Russian-Ukrainian conflicts are particularly acute in two areas: the Crimea and economic pressure. Russian domestic politics are evolving toward a more nationalistic and assertive agenda that will, at the very least, both damage Russian domestic reform and prolong the cold war with Ukraine. Ukrainian nationalists who have long called for Kiev to fully support the Crimean Tatars as a card against Russia might be tempted to claw back some of the autonomy rights granted to the Crimea. Nevertheless, although Crimean-Ukrainian relations are likely to improve in the aftermath of Kuchma's presidential victory, no Ukrainian leader will allow any threat to the territorial integrity of Ukraine. And President Kuchma has, perhaps ironically, adopted a harder line on the Crimea than his predecessor.

Meanwhile, Russian nationalists, both in the Crimea and Russia, have long argued that the Crimea (and Dniester Republic of Moldova) should be annexed to the Russian Federation. Russian leaders are unanimous in their view that the Dniester Republic and the Crimea should both have Russian bases and neither should belong to Moldova or Ukraine.

The Crimea has all the explosive potential of Bosnia-Herzegovina for a three-way civil war—that is, for conflict among the Russians, Ukrainians, and Muslim Tatars.[54] Perhaps the most dangerous aspect of the Crimean imbroglio is the unanimity among Russian leaders that Ukraine be denied the Crimea. "The Supreme Soviet of the Russian Federation correctly asserted the existence of the Crimean problem. This question has not disappeared with the disappearance of the Russian Supreme Soviet. There is absolutely no divergence of views in Russian political circles regarding Crimea. Absolutely none," Andranik Migranyan, Russian presidential adviser, told his Ukrainian hosts.[55]

In May and December 1992, the Russian parliament questioned the status of both the Crimea and the city of Sevastopol, while in July 1993 it actually declared Russian jurisdiction over the city, prompting denunciations from the Ukrainian and Crimean leaderships over what they regarded as renewed Russian territorial claims.[56] The Crimean question is connected to the status of the Black Sea Fleet and strongly influences Ukrainian attitudes toward nuclear weapons by sharpening Kiev's threat perceptions. Both former president Kravchuk and first deputy foreign minister Borys Tarasiuk have argued that the loss of the Crimea to Russia would end Ukraine's commitment to denuclearization.[57]

The July 1993 Russian parliamentary claim of sovereignty over Sevastopol by all of the deputies present (with only one abstaining) appreciably worsened Russian-Ukrainian relations and heightened Ukrainian security fears. Clearly the situation is dangerous because it reflects how even those who belong to the Yeltsin democratic camp can also react emotionally and historically to such questions as the Crimea. On the Ukrainian side, the claim was not only condemned by both president and parliament, but even called a "declaration of war" by some leading parliamentarians.[58] Even eastern Ukrainian-based political parties condemned this Russian claim because it would heighten anti-Russian sentiment within Ukraine.[59]

Ukrainian leaders regard Russia's threat of economic and political pressure as a more subtle attempt to integrate Ukraine into a new union under Russian domination. Russian vice premier Mikhail Poltoranin has argued that "Russian foreign policy vis-à-vis the former Soviet republics must be conducted through the use of such levers as natural oil and gas."[60]

Although it is difficult to gauge to what degree Ukraine's domestic economic crisis is more a product of mismanagement and lack of reform or external economic pressure, an economically weak Ukraine plays into Russian hands as a window of opportunity to exert pressure for reintegration. In his capacity as former premier, Kuchma, who cannot be accused of anti-Russian sentiments, complained during his period in office that "Russia is trying to bring about a full paralysis of the Ukrainian economy. . . . I cannot understand the Russian position. It is not motivated by economics. It can only be seen as some sort of pressure on Ukraine."[61]

As a result of the Zhirinovsky victory, Kozyrev admitted

that there would be changes in Russian foreign policy, "because it is necessary to take account of the problems that came to light during the election and the mood of the people." Kozyrev opposed the use of the "Zhirinovsky factor" by central Europeans and Balts to clamor for early entry into NATO. President Yeltsin's press spokesman, Viacheslav Kostikov, outlined Russia's tough new policies for 1994: "Undisputed emphasis in foreign policy will be given to protection of Russia's national interests and the rights of Russians and Russian-speaking people. . . . "

When British defense secretary Malcolm Rifkind warned of a serious risk of future war between Ukraine and Russia, more than half of the Ukrainian public agreed.[62] Indeed, after the Russian election results were announced, Kravchuk noted the "beginning of huge cataclysms in the world and in Europe, leading to carveups and partitions." What was alarming was that "millions of Russians voted for the slogan of a "great and indivisible Russia." Kravchuk repeatedly warned that any attempt to resurrect the USSR would end in bloodshed, and he accused Kuchma of favoring a revived union.

By early 1994 there was little to differentiate the policies of the democrats from that of the center-right, especially over demands to be given the right to "defend" the "Russian-speaking population" within the former USSR.[63] In a January 1994 poll of Moscow residents, 57 percent regretted the collapse of the former USSR, while only 25 percent viewed its collapse positively. By spring 1994, "much of Zhirinovsky's rhetoric is official Russian policy," backed by the majority of the centrist and democratic camp.[64] According to the Russian Ministry of Foreign Affairs, the strategic task of Russia is "to keep all Eurasian territory of the former Soviet Union if not under control then under strong influence."[65] President Kuchma has repeatedly stated that he will not be a "Russian vassal." Although Russian-Ukrainian relations in some areas will improve, in many areas outstanding problems will remain and may actually sharpen in the aftermath of the Chechnya crisis. By early 1995, two phases of "normalization" of Ukrainian-Russian relations—negotiations on the Black Sea Fleet and an interstate treaty—had still not been resolved.

Central and Eastern Europe

Ukraine's leaders, believing their country to be in a security vacuum, have looked to balance their dependence on Russia by enhancing cooperation with central Europe. Although Kravchuk rejected any recreation of the Warsaw Pact that would exclude Russia, at the late April 1993 CSCE meeting in Prague, the Ukrainian delegation proposed the creation of a collective security system (in effect, a *cordon sanitaire*). It was envisioned to include the Baltic States, Ukraine, Belarus, Moldova, Poland, Slovakia, the Czech Republic, Austria, Hungary, and possibly later Romania and Bulgaria. Russia was not on the list of proposed members.

Ukrainian security policy would aim to straddle both the CIS and central Europe. This two-track policy would satisfy the nationalists on one hand and the pro-CIS constituency on the other. The New Ukraine bloc of political groups and the Inter-Regional Bloc of Reforms, for example, consistently argued that, for economic considerations, Ukraine should remain in the CIS without signing the charter (the position also held by Kravchuk since late 1992, when the economic crisis came to a head).

The Ukrainian proposal for a collective security structure would have supplemented the CSCE framework. It would have been introduced in stages, first by members' declaring their interest in increasing security in the region, and then moving on to cooperation in security and the military. Key elements in the proposed structure would be renunciation of all territorial claims and the territorial integrity of borders, renunciation of the use of force, impermissability of deploying foreign troops on the territory of another state without the consent of that state, cooperation in conflict prevention, promotion of disarmament and arms controls, respect for national minority rights, and promotion of confidence-building measures. The new security structure would thus reflect Ukraine as a status quo power opposed to border changes.

Ukraine has signed treaties that renounce border changes with all of its central European neighbors, apart from Romania, and that also include guarantees for national minority rights.

Although the Transcarpathian oblast has a large Ukrainian majority, nationalist groups—for example, the Czech Republican
Party—claimed that it should be reincorporated within Czechoslovakia prior to 1992. With the disintegration of Czechoslovakia
in December 1992, this Czech claim was removed from the list
of potential border conflicts. Slovakia is unlikely to raise this
question itself because of the already large ethnic minorities on its
territories.

In June 1993, a Treaty of Good Neighborliness, Friendship,
and Cooperation was signed between Slovakia and Ukraine that,
like the treaties signed with Poland, Moldova, and Hungary,
ruled out border changes. Some Ukrainian nationalist groups,
however, have accused the Hungarians and Slovaks of supporting
Ruthenian separatism in Transcarpathia, a disputed ethnic border
group that many Ukrainians argue are linguistically and ethnically
Ukrainian.

In the Transcarpathian oblast, a large Hungarian minority
(150,000) that lives contiguous to the border has been granted
the status of a self-governing territory since December 1991.
Hungarian-Ukrainian relations have warmed appreciably since
1990, when Ukraine began making overtures to central Europe.
This has been helped by Budapest's view that Ukraine's treatment
of its ethnic Hungarian minorities is the best among all of its
neighbors. The Trans-Carpathian Hungarian Cultural Federation
has limited itself to socioeconomic, cultural, and educational
questions.[66]

Article 2 of the 1991 state treaty between Ukraine and Hungary contains a clause calling for the renunciation of mutual border claims now and in the future (including peaceful ones). Although approved by a large majority in the Hungarian
parliamentary foreign affairs committee, it was only ratified by
the Hungarian parliament in May 1993. Some members of the
then ruling Hungarian Democratic Forum (HDF) questioned the
inclusion of this clause, which, they believed, would set a prece-
dent for any future treaties negotiated with Romania and Slovakia. A primary factor in the expulsion of the nationalist wing
from the HDF, led by Istvan Csurka, was related to this question.

Ukrainian-Polish relations have rapidly evolved since 1990, a development supported by the majority of the Polish leadership. Despite the warm nature of these relations between Ukraine and the Visegrad group, some problems do exist.[67] The Poles were as frustrated as the Ukrainians at the "Russia-first" policy promoted by the United States toward the former USSR during 1992–1993 where Ukraine only entered Washington's radar screen on the question of nuclear weapons. Bogdan Borusewycz, head of the Polish-Ukrainian group in the Polish Sejm, then even argued that "Poland had been against the nuclear disarmament of Ukraine."[68]

The absence of national minorities as a point of conflict means that a Ukrainian-Polish conflict could only come about as a result of new imperialistic ambitions on the part of either partner or civil war and ethnic conflict in the former USSR leading to nationalist territorial demands upon Poland. But there are many problems with Ukrainian-Polish cooperation, including perceived instability in Ukraine, historical stereotypes, nuclear weapons, and nuclear power stations. In late 1992 a Polish opinion poll ranked Ukraine only below Germany as most "hostile" to Poland (higher than Russia and even Lithuania, where the Polish minority has been a source of friction between Vilnius and Warsaw). Disputes also exist over church property in border areas, while Polish nationalistic parties tend to be strongest in the southeastern region of the country.

The May 1992 Polish-Ukrainian Treaty on Good Neighborly, Friendly Relations and Cooperation also included the renunciation of all territorial claims now and in the future, renounced the use of force in relations between both parties, and stated that neither country would allow aggression to take place from its territory. President Lech Walesa argued after the signing of the treaty that "Poland needs a rich, strong and independent Ukraine" and that the new order in central Europe should be based on the principles of "equality, partnership and dialogue." President Lech Walesa's May 1993 visit to Ukraine further cemented this Ukrainian-Polish relationship, where he admitted that an "independent Ukraine is assurance for an independent Poland," and went on to argue, "I am convinced that there are prospects for cooperation in every sphere."

On the eve of the Polish visit of former Ukrainian foreign minister Zlenko in February 1994, Polish foreign minister Andrzej Olechowski stressed the importance of all-round cooperation between both countries. Ukrainian independence "is of strategic importance for Poland. . . . We are troubled by voices speaking about the special interests and special role of Russia in Ukraine. Such voices do not contribute to stability in Europe."[69] Poland would support Ukraine in international forums.

In the aftermath of the Zlenko visit, which came only two months after the victory of nationalists in the Russian elections, a communiqué stated that Poland and Ukraine would counter "the creation of new divisions in Europe, revival of hegemonistic tendencies and establishment of spheres of influence."

Besides Russia, only one other country has territorial claims against Ukraine–Romania. But historically, all of Ukraine's neighbors (except Belarus) have been in dispute with Kiev over border issues. Although unlike Russia, Romania does not threaten Ukraine's existence as an independent state.

Romanian-Ukrainian relations were harmed in 1990–1991 by territorial claims made by Bucharest toward Northern Bukovina, and Romania refused to recognize the results of the independence referendum in regions it claimed, calling upon Romanians living there to boycott it. The Romanian parliamentary declaration called Northern Bukovina "sacred Romanian lands" and "Romanian from time immemorial." Nevertheless, Romania could not become a real military threat to Ukraine.[70]

These factors have prevented the signing of a Friendship Treaty between Ukraine and Romania. In January 1993 the Romanian Ministry of Foreign Affairs called for finding the correct legal formulas to respect existing borders and settle such conflicts peacefully. He claimed that they did not have a "dream about a Greater Romania." On a visit to Ukraine in April 1993, the Romanian parliamentary speaker also stated, "We have come to Ukraine not to demand the return of territory but with the aim of developing friendship."

During a Ukrainian military exercise in August 1993, the only neighbor pointed to as a potential threat was Romania (not the more diplomatically difficult Russia, Poland, or Turkey). In

March 1994 a military cooperation agreement was signed between both countries. But deputy defense minister Ion Mircea Pascu gave it no particular significance, regarding it only as "routine." Problems with signing a political treaty continue, owing to Romanian territorial demands, and led to the cancellation of President Ion Iliescu's Ukrainian visit in 1993. Ukrainian-Romanian relations remain cool and are unlikely to improve in the short term, as also seen by the trading of recriminations over the treatment of their respective national minorities.

Romanian-Ukrainian relations are shaped by the Moldovan conflict and its future status. Although opinion polls and the March 1994 referendum currently show less than 10 percent of Moldovans in favor of early reunification with Romania,[71] both Ukraine and Hungary would be concerned by the creation of a "Greater Romania."[72] Reunification could lead to the influx of more than half a million Ukrainian refugees from right-bank Moldova to Ukraine, 59,000 of which have already crossed into Ukraine from the Dniester conflict.[73]

Ukraine faces a potential Russian military threat to its southern regions from the Dniester Republic. The Dniester Republic's leaders have openly admitted cooperating with pro-Russian secessionists in Ukraine's Donbas and Odesa regions with the hope of detaching them to create a *Novorossiya* (New Russia, the Tsarist term for southern Ukraine).[74] The further disintegration of Moldova could force it into reunification with Romania.

The combined military forces in the Dniester Republic are nearly 20,000, a sizable force that Russia hopes to use as a springboard to spread its influence in the Balkans. The 59th division of the former 14th Army based in the Dniester Republic is an 8,000-strong elite "Guards" force composed of armored, artillery, tactical missile, air defense, special forces, air reconnaissance, and engineering units. In addition, there are an additional 7,000 Dniester Republican Guard and 3,000 Russian peacekeeping forces, all of which are funded by the Russian Ministry of Defense.

These Russian armed forces are building houses, starting newspapers and television stations, and recruiting local residents. They seem to believe they will be staying in the Dniester Republic for a long time.[75] The military leaders of the republic believe that time is on their side; a post-Yeltsin Russia will eventually annex the region to Russia—a demand raised by General Alexander Lebed and Zhirinovsky.[76] Russian leaders are backing away from an autumn 1994 agreement to pull out Russian troops over a three-year period.

The gradual consolidation of Russian control over the Dniester Republic through its peacekeeping troops, the 14th Army, and the Dniester Republican force has been undertaken with the guidance of the Russian Ministry of Defense. Sergei Stankevych, former Russian state counsellor to President Yeltsin, has admitted that "every step of that Army's commander was authorized by the hierarchy of Russia's Ministry of Defence." This was undertaken to play the nationalist card domestically and to avoid losing "a valuable strategic outpost orientated toward the Balkans." Moscow initially held back for fear of offending the West.[77] But the West's policy of turning a blind eye to Russian imperialism in the former USSR gave Moscow the green light to provide unconditional support to the Dniester Republic.[78]

In early 1993 Moldova and Ukraine signed a comprehensive military agreement that in effect made them allies against Russian support to the secessionist Dniester Republic.[79] Ukraine supports Moldovan territorial integrity, opposes foreign intervention, and has called for the withdrawal of Russian armed forces from Moldova along the lines adopted by the December 1993 OSCE meeting. But Ukraine has failed to participate more directly in settling the Moldovan crisis because of its lack of a security policy toward the CIS.

Ukraine is also undertaking a more active policy by cutting communication lines to the 14th Army in the Dniester Republic, exchanging intelligence, training Moldovan officers, allowing Moldovan usage of Ukrainian ports, enhancing cooperation between Moldovan and Ukrainian Border Troops, and engaging in joint military exercises and air defenses. In addition, Kiev is attempting to detach Ukrainians from the Russian-speaking bloc in order to reduce the power base of the Dniester Republic's leaders.[80]

Ukraine's de facto military shield over Moldova may cause conflict with Russia, but Ukraine believes that its security interests will be best served by supporting Moldovan territorial integrity and freeing it of Russian influence. If Moldova were to disintegrate because the secessionist Dniester Republic is annexed to Russia, Ukraine would be forced to deal with the Dniester enclave on its border, which would bring it into direct military conflict with Russia.

By spring 1994 the nationalist phase in Moldovan politics ended with the victory of the centrist Agrarian Democratic Party in the February 27 elections. Those political forces that remain in favor of unification of Moldova and Romania only obtained 20 percent of the vote while the pro-Russian communist lobby obtained a similar amount. On March 6, the parliamentary vote was followed by a "People's Council" sociological poll that obtained a resounding 95.4 percent in favor of consolidating Moldovan independence (in contrast to unification with Romania).

These two events will have regional security ramifications. First, they have proved that the unification lobby is represented by only a minority of Moldovans, which will appease Ukrainian, Russian, and Hungarian concerns about the creation of a "Greater Romania."[81] Second, the Moldovans now have the same strategy vis-à-vis the CIS and Economic Union as the Ukrainians (the Moldovan parliament ratified its CIS and Economic Union membership after the elections).

Third, the new Moldovan leadership should encourage a domestic settlement of the separatist revolts in the Dniester and Gagauz regions with regional self-government, possibly on the basis of the CSCE plan adopted at its Rome meeting in December 1993. Finally, any settlement of Moldova's secessionist revolts will call the Russians' bluff. Moscow has constantly claimed that the 14th Army and Russian peacekeeping troops will be withdrawn after a settlement is reached. In contrast to Moscow, the Ukrainian ambassador has warmly praised Moldovan support for the revival of the Ukrainian minority and has demanded the withdrawal of Russian troops.[82]

During the first quarter of 1994, Belarus had returned to the status of a Russian *gubernia*, demanding a greater degree of integration than even the current Russian government was willing to provide. Belarus has a de facto status within the CIS similar to central Asia's. The conservatives within the Belarus parliament ousted the then reform-minded chairman of the Belarusian parliament Stanislau Shushkevich allegedly for "corruption," but in reality for his opposition to political-military integration with Russia.[83] The election of the populist Alexander Lukashenko as Belarusian president in summer 1994 will accelerate Belarus's integration with Russia (Lukashenko was endorsed by Russia's Zhirinovsky).

The regional security implications of Belarus's returning to the status of Russian protectorate are many. First, it has contributed to Ukrainian fears of encirclement (Dniester Republic, Crimea, and demands for changes to CFE limitations in the northern Caucasus) and heightened Ukrainian and Polish insecurity vis-à-vis Russian intentions. Second, economic and monetary union between Belarus and Russia will harm the latter's domestic reform program and place greater stress on reintegrating the remainder of the former USSR, major factors why Yevgenny Gaidar resigned from the Russian government in January 1994.

Third, Russian plans to establish 30 military bases within the former USSR outside Russia undoubtedly include Belarus. Indeed, an all-embracing military agreement was signed between both countries on March 11, 1994.[84] In the event of conflict between Ukraine and Russia, military bases in Belarus could be a threat to Ukraine's northwestern flank. Fourth, plans for a Baltic-Black Sea axis or even Central European Zone of Security and Cooperation are badly damaged by the loss of Belarus from the list of potential members. Ukraine is now cut off from the Baltic republics by Russian-dominated Belarus.

Ukraine has gradually expanded its bilateral relations with the three Baltic republics with whom it shares common security concerns. The Baltic Republics and Ukraine regularly protest the growing imperialistic direction of Russian security policy toward the former USSR, particularly demands to maintain forward military bases. Ukrainian-Estonian relations have accepted the continued legality of the October 27, 1923, treaty between both states. (Despite proclaiming itself as successor state to the former USSR, Russia has rejected the validity of the Estonian-USSR treaty of 1920.) The 1923 Ukrainian-Estonian treaty banning the presence of foreign troops on their respective territories has contemporary relevance.[85]

The Baltic republics and Ukraine were the first former Soviet states to join NATO's "Partnership for Peace," a membership they regard as a counterbalance to Russia. Lithuanian president Algirdas Brazauskas has also welcomed Ukraine's proposal for a Central European Security Zone that would include "economic and political cooperation and foreign policy interaction."[86] Relations, including military cooperation, have greatly expanded with Latvia, which has praised Ukrainian international diplomacy.

Turkey and the Middle East

Turkey will become an important strategic partner for Ukraine as a counterweight to Russia in the Black Sea region, the Balkans, and the Transcaucasus. Both Turkey and Ukraine oppose Russian demands for changes to CFE limits in the north Caucasus region.

Turkey will also play an important role in helping Ukraine lessen its dependency on Russian oil and gas supplies. Ukraine now plans to bring Iranian oil and gas through Turkey, bypassing the Transcaucasus, which has de facto returned to Russia's sphere of influence. This has cemented relations between Ukraine and Turkey and Iran. It has also brought Istanbul and Kiev closer in their security concerns about the revival of a new Russian empire, including mutual hostility toward Russian designs on the Crimea. Turkey, the main international backer of the Crimean Tatars, has opened a consulate in the Crimea. Turkey has also been very vocal in condemning Russian imperialism in the Caucasus.

The historical legal basis for Turkish-Ukrainian relations is the January 2, 1922, treaty updated by the signing of a Treaty on Friendship and Good Neighborly Relations in May 1992.[87] Military and security cooperation have ensued between both countries, including the exchange of intelligence and Turkish support for Ukrainian membership in NATO. The geopolitical situation made military and technical cooperation between both countries essential, according to a communiqué released during the visit of the Turkish defense minister to Ukraine.[88] In mid-

April 1994, Ukraine and Turkey signed a security cooperation agreement that included joint struggle against organized crime, terrorism, and separatism.

Ukraine and Turkey both look to the Black Sea Economic Cooperation Agreement (BSECA) as a vehicle to enhance their bilateral relations. Kiev and Istanbul have supported proposals for the demilitarization of the Black Sea and the creation of a nuclear-free zone, both policies directed primarily at Russia. Both Turkey and Ukraine backed calls to establish a Parliamentary Assembly within the parameters of the BSECA, at the same time as Ukraine has been lukewarm about the CIS equivalent structure.[89] The two main active member states of the BSECA are Turkey and Ukraine.[90]

Ukraine proposed security proposals for the Black Sea region at a meeting of the BSECA in Kiev in November 1993. At its Tbilisi meeting the following May, these security proposals were further discussed, much to the consternation of Russia, which sees it as a means whereby former Soviet republics can reduce their dependency on Russia and articulate non-Eurasian orientations. Ukrainian security proposals for the BSECA include banning the offensive capabilities of Black Sea navies, limiting the frequency of naval exercises in the Black Sea, signing nonaggression treaties in the Black Sea region, and issuing declarations on the inviolability of the borders of Black Sea states.[91]

Both Turkey and Ukraine have supported the territorial integrity of states in the Black Sea region (Armenia, Russia's Caucasian ally, has been accused by the Turkish media of training PKK Kurdish separatists). The Turks have expressed support for Ukrainian territorial integrity and sovereignty over the Crimea and have promoted a peaceful resolution to the Gagauz question in Moldova (in contrast to Russian support for the Dniester Republic and 14th Army). Other security proposals provide for the detailing of naval activities and for the inadmissibility of members who utilize their naval forces against other BSECA members or allow their territory to be used for the launch of aggression against other members.

Ukraine has developed bilateral economic relations with Iran, particularly with respect to alternate non-Russian sources of energy. Ukraine is regarded as a new gateway for Iranian goods to Europe. An agreement of mutual understanding on economic and political cooperation was signed during President Kravchuk's visit to Iran in April 1992. The transit of oil from Iran to Ukraine through Azerbaijan was shelved in favor of Turkey. Iran is interested in Ukrainian technology, industrial know-how, and nuclear energy technology.

The Ukrainian rapprochement with Iran also occurred during Kiev's growing disillusionment with the West, views that were backed by Tehran. When former parliamentary speaker Pliushch visited Tehran, he stressed the need for Iran to develop closer ties with Ukraine and Central Asia that would "help consolidate their independence." Iran should then "further consolidate (Ukrainian) independence."[92] Politically Ukraine and Iran also share the same fears and suspicions of Russian imperialism in Tajikistan and the Transcaucasus. Although there have been persistent Ukrainian denials, undoubtedly Ukraine has exported some military spare parts and equipment to Iran, an area of trade that is likely to increase.[93]

Asia

Ukraine and the Central Asian republics have diametrically opposed policies vis-à-vis CIS integration. But some common ground does nevertheless exist between them. Within the CIS, Ukraine and the Central Asian republics of Kazakhstan, Kyrgyzstan, and Uzbekistan have stood firm together against Russian demands for dual citizenship for Russian minorities and have rejected Moscow's claim to be the "protector" of Russian speakers, which they accuse of interference in their domestic affairs.[94] Ukraine's success in obtaining security assurances and financial compensation for denuclearization has also encouraged the Kazakh leadership to demand similar treatment. Ukraine and Kazakhstan are likely to cooperate in the Baykanur space station.[95]

During President Nursultan Nazarbayev's visit to Ukraine in January 1994, a declaration signed between both countries condemned aggressive nationalistic patriotism and imperialistic chauvinism, clearly references to Russia. It also went on to criticize outside support for destabilization and the aggravation of interethnic conflicts, coupled with attempts to establish "spheres of influence."[96] Nazarbayev also complained of Western appeasement of Russia that risked "encouraging chauvinism and helping fascism in Russia," statements Kiev supports.[97] Kazakhstan and Ukraine have similar problems vis-à-vis Russian intentions toward northern Kazakhstan and the Donbas-Crimea, respectively.

Ukraine and India have developed close economic and military relations since the disintegration of the former USSR. A Treaty on Friendship and Cooperation was signed as early as March 27, 1992. Other agreements have been signed between Ukraine and India dealing with trade, economics, and scientific-technical issues.

Military cooperation will undoubtedly play an additionally important part in Ukrainian-Indian trade. In the words of Kravchuk on his return from India, "Our cooperation with India does not begin from zero. Around 60 percent of the ties which existed between India and the former Soviet Union came through Ukraine."[98] India and Ukraine hold similar views about separatism and threats to their territorial integrity (Kashmir-Crimea) as well as refusal to accept international pressure on security questions.[99]

Ukraine's other important partner in Asia is China. In that country on an official visit, Kravchuk called it a "strategic partner." Ukraine is interested in the Chinese experience of economic reform, while China is interested in Ukraine's scientific-technological expertise.[100]

Trade between both countries, low because of the economic crisis and slow pace of reforms in Ukraine, has mostly occurred through barter. Economic cooperation was expanded in April 1994 with a combination of barter, cash transactions, and the settling of accounts in a third country. China is also interested in Ukrainian technology and military hardware. A large potential exists for technical cooperation, trade, and joint ventures between both countries. Bilateral economic relations would be developed by the Ukrainian-Chinese Commission on Trade and Economic Cooperation, and China has agreed to give Ukraine a loan of $5 million. The trade potential between both countries, according to defense minister Shmarov, is $4 billion (in 1993 total trade amounted to only $679 million).

Chinese-Ukrainian relations have progressed faster on the political level. Ukraine has supported China's position on Taiwan in return for Beijing's backing for Ukrainian "independence, sovereignty and territorial integrity." Both China and Ukraine have historically been in conflict with Russia and thus understand each other's security concerns. The communiqué released during Kravchuk's visit to China spoke of their joint "struggle against hegemonism and diktat in international relations."[101] In May 1993 China agreed to extend a security guarantee to Ukraine if it ratified START I, although Beijing did not pressure Kiev to denuclearize. Some Chinese circles even regarded Ukraine's retention of nuclear weapons as a useful counterbalance to Russia.[102]

Conclusion

During 1992, Ukraine aimed to establish its foreign policy presence internationally. By the following year, it had elaborated an intellectual basis for the main direction of its foreign policy, coupling it with a military doctrine. Ukraine was also preoccupied during this period with state and nation building (unlike Russia, which quickly dropped this in favor of the reintegration of the former USSR).

Economic and political crisis has increased the regional divisions in the Ukrainian leadership and society, which has slowed Ukraine in formulating clear national interests and priorities. They are beginning to take shape, and Ukraine's formulation of foreign policy is becoming more professional. In foreign policy, Ukraine has little choice but to continue its dual-track approach toward integration in the CIS and elsewhere, despite the election of President Kuchma. On the one hand, Ukraine will not reject integration with the CIS, but it will remain limited to full membership in the economic sphere. On the other hand, Ukraine's national interests dictate that integration continue with Western structures (NATO, EU, and the Council of Europe). Like the

Baltic republics, Ukraine will play a high-profile role in Western structures while refraining from becoming a full member of any Eurasian Union (unlike Belarus).

Two regions that will remain priorities for Ukraine are central Europe and the Black Sea region. Ukraine would like to join the Visegrad group and Central European Initiative while quietly dropping its own Security Zone. Turkey and the Black Sea region will continue to remain a central focus of Ukrainian foreign and security policy, owing to Russian intervention in the Caucasus and Crimea and with the Black Sea Fleet. These factors are likely to bring Turkish and Ukrainian interests even closer, as will the issue of energy supplies to Ukraine and improved economic ties.

The main foreign policy concern and external threat to Ukrainian independence is, and will remain for the foreseeable future, Russia. Although Romania harbors territorial claims, they are regionally based and do not represent a real military threat to Ukrainian independence. Faced until recently by a largely indifferent West and a sympathetic, but cautious, central Europe, Ukraine's sense of isolation grew, placing it under greater pressure to reunite with Russia. An isolated Ukraine would provide fertile ground for those favoring a nationalist, authoritarian solution, and would swell the ranks of the pronuclear lobby within the country.

The "cold war" between Ukraine and Russia may decline with the election of President Kuchma, but tension will remain as Kiev feels growing pressure to reintegrate with the CIS politically, militarily, and economically. Although Russian armed forces could not, in their present state, launch a full-scale offensive against Ukraine, Russian interventionist support for separatist regions, in a manner similar to that pursued in the Transcaucasus, is likely to continue. The Georgian scenario of using Abkhazia as a lever for reintegration within the Russian sphere of influence could be a test run for Ukraine, as it is unlikely to go the Belarusian way, cap in hand back to Moscow. Russian policy toward the republics of the former USSR is increasingly imperialist and confrontational.

This evolution of Russian security policy toward the political right will continue; there is already little practical difference between Russian political groups over the question of reintegrating the former USSR. Republics, such as Ukraine, can choose between two types of reintegration. The current form uses support for separatism, federalization, and economic pressure to establish a CIS confederation—that is, Russia surrounded by a rim of non-Russian satellites in a relationship similar to that between the USSR and Eastern Europe during the cold war. The other form, which is promoted by Russian nationalists, would create a new USSR by force.[103] There is no longer an influential Russian political constituency, which existed in 1990–1992, that rejects empire in favor of nation building.

Even this distinction between the current center-right "pragmatists" and "national patriots" is becoming blurred, as witnessed by the Chechnya crisis in winter 1994–1995. Shumeyko, chairman of the Russian Federation Council and CIS Interparliamentary Assembly, has welcomed the Kazakh president's proposal to transform the CIS into a "Eurasian union," a matter discussed at the autumn 1994 summit of the CIS.

Sergei Shakhray, leader of the center-right Party for Russian Unity and Accord, which models itself on Western European conservative parties, has offered to provide organization and financial backing for discussion of a draft confederation agreement that would lead to a new Union.[104] At the CIS's April 1994 summit, Ukraine was again at loggerheads in opposing the revival of the former USSR. A senior Ukrainian diplomat was quoted as saying that if Ukraine signed the CIS Charter and became a full member of its Economic Union, "this will be the beginning of the end of Ukrainian statehood."[105] President Kuchma will be forced to take into account the strong domestic pressure against full integration with Russia/CIS, which, if ignored, would lead to large-scale domestic instability.

As early as February 1993, President Yeltsin backed calls by the Ministry of Defense for the establishment of 30 military bases within the non-Russian republics of the former USSR, backed up by a presidential decree in April 1994. The only republics exempted from this plan were the Baltic Republics and Ukraine. Possible exceptions would be the Black Sea Fleet base of Sevastopol and Skrunda Radar station in Latvia.[106]

Until now Ukraine has largely escaped these Russian policies applied in the Transcaucasus with such success because of its moderate leadership, good record on national minority rights, and its membership in the CIS. But Ukraine will remain vulnerable for a long time to come, given its dependence on Russian energy supplies and the difficulty of implementing any alternative plans.

Russian foreign policy toward the republics of the former USSR will continue to remain integrationist, facilitated by the domestic weakness of countries such as Ukraine.[107] If "National Patriots," such as Zhirinovsky, come to power in Russia, a full-blown conflict, perhaps ignited by the continuing dispute over the Crimea, cannot be ruled out with Ukraine. Ukrainian and Russian national interests diverge both within and outside the former USSR; therefore, the possibility of future conflicts in other geographic regions exists if, and when, Ukraine is more self-confident and assertive in its national interests.

Many Russians and political groups find it difficult to accept Ukraine's independence as well as its control over the Donbas and Crimea. There is a deep and widely held belief within the Russian elite, which is, of course, highly irritating to Ukrainian leaders, that Ukrainian independence is somehow "temporary" and thus reunification is inevitable in the future. Speaking in Warsaw, President Yeltsin's political adviser Sergei Stankevich warned Poland to reduce its ties to Ukraine, arguing that Ukraine and Belarus fall within the "Russian sphere of influence."[108]

4

Military and Nuclear Policy

For the historical reasons outlined in chapter 1, Ukraine focused on building up its armed forces. This policy choice was best suited to ensuring a gradual nationalization of the former Soviet armed forces on Ukrainian territory. Ukraine's nationalization of a large proportion of these forces broke the back of the once formidable Soviet military machine and prevented any internal military threat to the Ukrainian drive to independence after December 1991.[1] This policy, at the very least, produced a sizable group of officers that supported Ukrainian independence while neutralizing the potential threat from the remainder of them.[2]

The nationalization of former Soviet armed forces in Ukraine and the large number of officers serving outside Ukraine within the CIS will pose a severe social cost in their integration into society and the economy as the armed forces are reduced in size and transferred to a professional basis.[3]

An exception to the smooth nationalization of the former Soviet armed forces is the Black Sea Fleet and its division between Russia and Ukraine; a solution is likely to continue to be problematical because of its close connection to possession of the Crimea and development of Russian security policy in a more imperialistic direction. The Black Sea Fleet has no strategic value; its importance only lies within the realm of denying it to the other side and any proceeds from possible sales of equipment.

This chapter argues that Russia's claim to that portion of the Black Sea located in Ukraine, as well as the city of Sevastopol, after obtaining the other three fleets of the former USSR, is not conducive to promoting regional stability, overcoming Ukrainian insecurity, or improving Ukrainian-Russian relations.

Ukrainian nuclear policy has not been consistent. During the course of 1992–1993, however, Ukraine's mixed ad hoc responses to developments in Russia could have led Kiev to become a full-fledged nuclear power. In 1994 Ukraine ratified START I and the NPT in exchange for widely encompassing security assurances (not guarantees as Kiev had demanded) and financial compensation.

This chapter points to the key factors influencing this trend and the role of key groups and personalities toward nuclear weapons. The major driving forces behind the trend toward retaining nuclear weapons are Ukrainian insecurity, inferiority complex, and suspicion of the motives of the outside world, which, for many within the Ukrainian leadership, is a self-fulfilling prophecy. Retention of some nuclear weapons by Kiev would only serve to worsen Ukrainian security and increase its isolation. Yet, ironically, facing these two factors (insecurity and isolation) is what Ukraine fears most.

This chapter also analyzes the key elements available to formulate Ukrainian security policy and surveys the Ukrainian inheritance of the former Soviet military. It looks at points of dispute between Ukraine and Russia over this military inheritance, in particular the Black Sea Fleet and nuclear weapons. Finally, the chapter identifies the main trends of these elements in future Ukrainian security policy.

Soviet Military Inheritance: Conventional, Naval, and Nuclear

Armed Forces

When the USSR disintegrated, Ukraine inherited formidable Soviet military assets, including 30 percent of the equipment west of the Ural mountains in 1991 and 750,000 personnel. Of all the republics of the former USSR, only Russia and Ukraine inherited the resources to equip large armed forces. Ukraine inherited elements of the former Soviet Ground Forces, Tactical and Strategic Air Force, Black Sea Fleet, Air Defence Force, and Strategic Missile Force. Ukraine possesses the second largest armed forces in Europe after Russia, which will remain the case until at least the end of the decade. The Conventional Forces Europe (CFE) Treaty benefits Ukraine by reinforcing Ukrainian control over a large volume of high quality equipment, although thousands of items will have to be destroyed. The Ukrainian share of the treaty limited equipment from the former Soviet armed forces is nearly a third.

The military equipment inherited by Ukraine will be more than sufficient to both equip the new armed forces and export some items for hard currency (both legally and illegally by corrupt elements within the Ministry of Defense).[4] Ukraine inherited more than 6,500 tanks, including the most modern T-80, T-72, and T-64. Other pieces of equipment include 7,500 armored personnel carriers, 5,000 support vehicles, and more than 3,300 artillery pieces. By the end of 1995, the CFE limits Ukraine to reducing the number of tanks by one-third and armored personnel carriers by one-sixth. This will still leave formidable numbers of tanks and other items in Ukrainian hands, especially as the CFE allows Ukraine to increase its artillery pieces.

Although Ukraine inherited a large volume of relatively modern equipment, it is located away from what Kiev regards as the main threats to its territorial integrity. The bulk of the former Soviet forces were located in the Carpathian military district, whereas the main threat is from Russia in the East or from separatist conflict in Crimea in the South. There are no Ukrainian armed forces on the Russian-Ukrainian border, although nationalist groups have demanded the transfer of the bulk of units to this region, which would be highly costly, time consuming, and provocative to Russia (and some eastern Ukrainians).

In the meantime, Kiev has dispatched six guard detachments of Border Troops to the Belarusian and Russian frontiers, creating an additional southeastern (Kharkiv) directorate in addition to the already existing former Soviet southwestern (L'viv) and southern (Odesa) ones. In addition, the three military districts were abolished in November 1992 and replaced by western and southern operational (or tactical) commands.[5] The Central Defence Ministry Board became the successor to the Kiev district.[6] These tactical commands would consist of army and mechanized corps and mechanized tank divisions and brigades as well as military training centers.

In the southern district, military restructuring will create army corps and mechanized brigades to improve mobility and rapid deployment to the missions assigned to them.[7] In March 1993 the armed forces in the southern operational command began regular exercises with the participation of Navy Marines, Border Troops, and the National Guard.[8] Presumably the importance of the southern district rests on the closeness of the Moldovan and Crimean disputes. Any Russian control of the Crimea, or Russian naval bases in Sevastopol, would make defense of southern Ukraine more difficult militarily.

Although the military equipment inherited by Ukraine is large, a major factor in its nationalization was merely to deny its possession by Russia. The equipment is thus unlikely to be incorporated within Ukrainian military planning. With the defense budget under pressure from the huge budget deficit, economic crisis, and hyperinflation, few funds are available for spare parts or maintenance. Air force training had been suspended because one-third of aircraft were out of order. Repair was impossible because there was not even enough fuel to check the engines.

The government budget for 1993 only covered salaries for the armed forces; it had no provision for training, modernization, or redeployment. Only 10 percent of the budgetary requirements for the armed forces were allocated in early 1994. The Ministry of Defense had requested over 64 trillion *karbovanets* (coupons, approximately $1.8 billion), but was only allocated a fraction of this figure.[9] Limited fuel supplies have prevented training exercises and the maintenance of operational effectiveness.

Black Sea Fleet

The Black Sea Fleet comprised 26 percent of the former Soviet Navy ships and 7 percent of its submarines, primarily based in the Ukrainian ports of Sevastopol and Odesa, with smaller bases in Poti, Georgia, and Novorossisk, Russia. It was only the third in size of the four Soviet fleets, three of which Russia inherited completely, but still the twelfth largest in the world. Its primary role was to defend the Black Sea coast, a task that would remain part of Ukrainian military policy. In total, the Black Sea Fleet included 18 submarines, 39 principal combat and 60 patrol and coastal ships, as well as 30 mine warfare and 16 amphibious craft. The Mykolayiv shipyards were the sole location for the building of aircraft carriers in the former USSR (which were taken over by Kiev in November 1991).[10]

The Black Sea Fleet also possessed a large ground and aviation force. This included a Naval Infantry Brigade based in Sevastopol equipped with 60 artillery and over 100 armored vehicles. Initially the former USSR attempted to skirt around the CFE treaty by reclassifying the ground forces division in Simferopol as a "Coastal Defence Division." This division is very modern with nearly 300 tanks and 600 armored vehicles. Since summer 1992 it has been under Kiev's control and hence a powerful weapon for asserting control over the Crimean peninsula. The Black Sea Fleet also possessed more than 400 combat aircraft (fighters and bombers) from six bases – three in the Crimea and three elsewhere in Ukraine. Another 100 helicopters compliment the fleet.

The cost of building a Ukrainian navy will be high, dependent upon the economy and a medium- to long-term program. Former Ukrainian Rear Admiral Boris Kozhyn (who was replaced by Vice Admiral Volodymyr Bezkorovainy in October 1993) outlined highly ambitious plans for a future Ukrainian navy, separate to its share of the Black Sea Fleet.[11] The Ukrainian navy would include a total of 100 ships with 40,000 men, including missile cruisers, multipurpose patrol ships, missile ships, and minesweepers. He rejected the view that it would possess nuclear weapons, although Admiral Volodymyr S. Pylypenko disagreed, calling those who were for a nuclear-free Ukrainian navy "either stupid, ill or even playing unserious games."[12] More realistic plans have been suggested by former defense minister Morozov – a total of 14 ships by 1998.

These relatively ambitious, and probably unrealistic, plans would in the short term give the Ukrainian navy a force size of

40 and 25 percent respectively of the former Soviet Black Sea Fleet's manpower and vessels. This would be less than the United Kingdom/French average of more than 60,000 men in their navies, but still quite high for a country with an economic crisis as acute as Ukraine's. In light of this crisis, the military leadership has resorted to pleading with local leaders of each oblast to pay for the construction of one vessel each (which, if fully implemented, would yield a total force of no more than 25 craft).

In the meantime, the Black Sea Fleet will either be transferred to Russia completely or the current stalemate will continue; it has little, if any, value to Ukraine while the majority of officers are oriented toward Russia. Ukraine could not take over the entire fleet itself because of the pro-Russian sentiments of the bulk of its officer corps.

Air Force

Ukraine's inheritance of a substantial air force comprised Long-Range Aviation (strategic) planes, tactical planes, interceptors of the Air Defence Force, helicopters within the Ground Force units, and the large number of aircraft assigned to the Black Sea Fleet. All of the 22 modern TU-160 Blackjack bombers based at Priluki, together with 21 TU-95 H-16 Bear 2 bombers at Uzin, were inherited by Ukraine (except for those that defected to Russia in early 1992). Each Blackjack and Bear-H can carry 12 and 15 Air-Launched Cruise Missiles (ALCMs) with a total of 192 and 224 warheads, respectively. Ukraine also inherited all of the *Midas* tanker aircraft used to fuel these strategic aircraft. Kiev plans that the tanker fleet are to be used as commercial air freight aircraft from 1994, while the strategic bombers could be converted for use in "ecological patrols under the aegis of the UN" (sic!). The TU-95 bombers are likely to be kept, while the TU-160 aircraft will be recycled.

The total number of aircraft inherited by Ukraine thus includes 150 bombers, 180 strike aircraft, 120 reconnaissance and electronic warfare aircraft, 510 air defense fighters, and nearly 800 training aircraft. Within the CFE limits, the total number of aircraft is to be reduced by more than a third. Ukraine's share of the helicopters from the former Soviet inventory includes nearly 700 attack, support, and unarmed helicopters subordinated to Ground Forces and nearly 100 to the Air Force. The CFE ceiling of 285 attack (MI-24 *"Hind"*) helicopters can be raised to 330 by 1995, which will be useful for rapid deployment forces in the event of future low intensity conflict in Ukraine.

Ukraine announced plans in 1993 to amalgamate the Air Force and Air Defence Forces. After the appointment of Lieutenant-General Volodymyr Antonets as commander of the combined forces, all six members of the Air Force Military Council resigned. One of their reasons for opposing Antonets is his support for the Union of Ukrainian Officers and other nationalist structures within the armed forces.[13]

Nuclear Weapons

Ukraine inherited the largest number of strategic forces outside Russia at two missile bases—Khmel'nyts'kyy (130 Russian-built SS-19s with 6 warheads each) and Pervomaisk (40 Ukrainian-produced SS-24s with 10 warheads each), all silo-based with a total of 1,180 warheads (coupled with potential extra warheads in storage).[14] The 43rd Strategic Rocket Army was disbanded by Kiev in November 1992, then reorganized consisting of 20,000 servicemen mainly drawn from Ukraine. A secret military order in July 1993 placed all "C" units (special troops of the Strategic Rocket Troops, or SRT, involved in storage and repair of nuclear warheads) under Ukrainian jurisdiction.[15] The SRT have been forced to take the Ukrainian loyalty oath; those that refused were transferred to Russia.

At the time of the demise of the former USSR, the West was most concerned about tactical nuclear weapons, which were more likely to fall into the hands of extremist groups in the event of general chaos and civil war or to be sold abroad. Whereas Russian interest lay in exaggerating those forces it defined as "strategic" within the former Soviet armed forces, Ukraine's interests lay in narrowly defining those units it regarded as strategic. Because some of the vessels had tactical nuclear weapons, Russia therefore continued to argue that the entire Black Sea Fleet was strategic. This encouraged Ukraine to transfer tactical nuclear weapons to Russia from the Ground Forces and Black Sea Fleet as soon as possible so that these units could no longer, in Kiev's eyes, be classified as strategic.

The 3,905 modern tactical nuclear missiles (14 percent of the CIS total) were therefore transferred to Russia two months ahead of schedule by May 1992, after a halt in the transfer in March, which led to strong U.S. and Russian protests.[16] Ukraine did not demand compensation for these weapons until a year later.

Although Ukraine may keep the SS-24 missiles and ALCMs in the short to medium terms, it is difficult to see how they would become a full deterrent in their own right without the remaining infrastructure required for this purpose. The SS-24 missiles will be obsolete within 15 years; if Ukraine wanted to continue being a nuclear power after that period, it would need a huge investment in resources. Four items crucial to modernizing Ukrainian nuclear weapons are missing from Ukraine's military industrial complex: a reprocessing plant to supply enriched uranium for warheads, a warhead test site, a missile test range, and communications satellites.

Conventional and Naval Forces: Policies and Conflicts

Military Doctrine[17]

In November 1991, Ukraine was the first of the former Soviet republics to declare its intention to draw up a military doctrine within three months' time. This term proved to be unrealistic; it only later became apparent that military doctrine is but one section of an all-embracing national security policy.

The ratification by the Ukrainian parliament on October 19, 1993, of its military doctrine not only reflected the radicalization of Ukrainian security policy since its first draft in May 1992 but also brought it into further collision with Russia. The Russian military doctrine institutionalized its Monroe/Karaganov Doctrine as well as added further pressure upon Ukraine to denuclearize.

The second revised draft of the military doctrine was adopted by a closed session of parliament almost without discussion in October 1993.[18] Nuclear disarmament was made conditional on Western security guarantees, but it continued to define START I (in contrast to Russia and the United States) as not covering 46 SS-24 missiles based in Ukraine. The newly ratified doctrine also noted that Ukraine became the "owner" of nuclear weapons through "historical circumstances," but nevertheless will never employ the threat to use nuclear weapons in its security policy (unlike the newly adopted Russian doctrine).

In addition, the statement "Ukraine does not consider any state as its adversary" was changed to read, "Ukraine will consider its potential adversary to be a state whose consistent policy constitutes a military danger to Ukraine, leads to interference into its internal affairs, encroachments upon its territorial integrity and national interests." In other important aspects, the newly ratified Ukrainian military doctrine

- recognizes that the national security concerns of states are interconnected
- opposes the stationing of foreign troops on its territory and in other countries without their consent (e.g., Moldova, Baltic Republics, and so on)
- continues to support a "non bloc status," but stands for the creation of an all-European security system and "regional security systems"
- characterizes the use of nuclear weapons as "inadmissible"
- states that Ukraine will become a non-nuclear state "in the future."

Border Troops and the National Guard

The easiest Soviet units to nationalize were the Border Troops and internal Ministry of Interior (MVD) Special Purpose Troops. Given that they were relatively small and often recruited locally, they aroused little dispute with Moscow.

Ukraine inherited 17,000 former Soviet Border Troops, which will be increased to 36,000. Until the end of 1992, the Border Troops continued to defend only the former Soviet external frontiers,[19] but from January 1993 Border Troops were also placed on the Russian and Belorussian frontiers with Ukraine, the extra numbers for the six detachments transferred from the armed forces. This was followed from April 1993 on with customs and border controls on all air communication routes to Ukraine from the CIS, whose citizens now need a visa to enter Ukraine.

Ukrainian borders are among the longest in Europe at nearly 7,600 kilometers. One reason for introducing Border Troops on the Russian frontier was to prevent the use of Ukraine as a transit route for narcotics, weapons, and illegal immigrants to western and central Europe. During 1992, more than 1,000 Third World refugees with Russian visas were caught attempting to cross Ukraine's borders with central Europe; 1,000 weapons and 4 kilos of narcotics were confiscated. Strengthening Ukrainian border controls with the CIS has thus been welcomed by Ukraine's central European neighbors.

MVD Troops created the core for the National Guard, which would have functions similar to paramilitary units in western Europe, such as the French *Compagnie Republicains de Securite* or Italian *Carabinieri* under parliamentary (and not presidential or Ministry of Defense) control. Kiev also maintained some of the former MVD units as Internal Troops (as traditional prison and camp guards), Convoy Defense, and Railway Troops.

Initially, the Crimean leaders opposed the presence of the National Guard in the autonomous republic. But in October 1992, after the various disorders and occupation of the Crimean parliament by a Tatar mob, they consented; a sizable contingent is now based in Simferopol, capital of the Crimean autonomous republic.

The National Guard's current strength of nearly 20,000 is planned to become 30,000 to 50,000. Its aims include assisting the Border Troops in defending Ukraine's territorial integrity (the first action of which was to help seal the Moldovan-Ukrainian border in March 1992 after conflict erupted in the Dniester Republic), responding to emergencies, guarding government buildings and embassies, and serving as guards of honor.[20] Although the National Guard was not initially geared to maintain standard law and order, by spring 1993 its duties had been expanded to include this responsibility when it joined the *"Berkut"* riot police in assisting the regular militia. Joint National Guard and Militia patrols throughout Ukraine, including the Crimea, were reported as successful in suppressing organized crime and confiscating an assortment of weapons.[21] In the event of martial law, they would play a leading role (as in Poland in December 1981).

The Border Troops and National Guard were the easiest to nationalize and would be the backbone (together with the airborne and *Spetsnaz* forces) of any defensive operation against internal armed separatists or an external offensive operation against Ukraine. A certain number of the reduced armed forces will be relocated to these units, which are likely to be more appropriate to challenge current low-intensity security problems. The number of planned National Guard divisions has substantially increased in response to growing separatism. But the cost of relocating and positioning Border Troops on the border with Russia will be high and time-consuming.

Conventional Armed Forces

In contrast to other regions of the former USSR, Ukraine adopted a largely consistent and, by Soviet standards, radical policy toward conventional armed forces immediately after the 24 August 24, 1991, declaration of independence. Ukraine's nationalization of three-quarters of a million Soviet armed service personnel along with military equipment was largely successful—with no reported military clashes or anarchical disintegration of weaponry into the hands of warlords, such as happened in the Transcaucasus.

The transfer of equipment to Ukrainian jurisdiction occurred peacefully and orderly, except in the small number of cases where defections occurred or equipment was transferred to

Russia. Ukraine's sometimes abrasive policies did contribute to friction with Russia and within the CIS. But with hindsight it prevented the continuation of foreign military bases on its territory, which could have fueled future separatism, armed revolt, and instability (as in Moldova).

Throughout early 1992, Ukraine administered an oath to conscripts and officers that called for loyalty to the "peoples of Ukraine" (not the Ukrainian nation). It was deliberately phrased to ensure a high rate of acquiescence by non-Ukrainian officers. At that time, according to the General Staff of the former USSR, 45 percent of troops in Ukraine were Ukrainian and 40 percent Russian (including 75,000 Russian officers). Upwards of 80 percent of troops, including 600 officers of the Black Sea Fleet, took the Ukrainian oath of loyalty.

Those who refused to take the loyalty oath were repatriated to Russia or other republics (a demand made by radical groups, such as the Union of Ukrainian Officers), while increasingly large numbers of the 300,000 Ukrainians serving outside the republic demanded to be allowed to return. Reportedly 30,000 to 50,000 non-Ukrainian officers are still serving in the armed forces in Ukraine, primarily in the Black Sea Fleet and Strategic Rocket Troops. A total of more than 10,000 officers refused to take the Ukrainian oath. Of these, 3,500 opted to stay in Ukraine and left the armed forces, while the remainder left the republic during 1992–1993.

A strategy that appealed to the fears of the former Soviet armed service personnel on Ukrainian territory helped induce them to take the oath. The highly favorable Ukrainian "Law on Social and Legal Defence of Servicemen and Members of Their Family" was adopted in late December 1991, the first such law in the former USSR.[22] It was believed, correctly, that the major concerns of officers were social–apartments, families, pension rights, and employment opportunities. The Ukrainian law helped to alleviate these fears, thereby encouraging the bulk of the officers to take the Ukrainian oath. But whether the Ukrainian economy will have sufficient resources not to renege on this law is doubtful. Throughout Ukraine, 73,000 officers are still without apartments, and another 100,000 officers will return to Ukraine from the former USSR by 1995.[23]

The successful nationalization of the former Soviet armed forces on Ukrainian territory will create tremendous social problems in the medium to long term and place great strains on the economy and government budget. Competition for housing could lead to conflict between those officers who can show that they are the most "patriotic," squeezing out undesirables and inflaming nationalist passions over scarce resources. A Center for the Professional Retraining of Servicemen was opened in Kiev as a joint project of the Defense and Educational Ministries, Employment Agency, and a German company in March 1993,[24] together with a Ukrainian Officers Bank,[25] but these initiatives will only dent the problem. Military service remains highly unpopular – only a third of young people of call-up age are registering – as well as dangerous (209 Ukrainian service personnel were killed through crime or accidents in the first six months of 1993 while more than 500 committed suicide in 1994, many of them officers).[26] Few of those who do not register as conscripts are tried in court.[27]

By 1995 Ukraine's armed forces are to be reduced to 450,000 from their high figure of 750,000, and by the end of the. decade to a quarter of a million – a task that will be difficult, if not impossible, to fulfill. These reductions will depend on developments in Russia, but also on the state of the economy.

Ukraine's rapid establishment of armed forces was coupled with an overhaul of former Soviet military academies, reflecting Ukraine's need to build new loyalties to the newly independent state within the officer corps. During 1992–1993 Ukraine inherited a large number of the most prestigious military academies in the former USSR, including Armed Forces, KGB, Border Troops, MVD, Strategic Rocket Troops, and Special Military Schools for Third World students. The 1992 decree on military education drew upon precommunist Ukrainian traditions, streamlined the large number of former Soviet academies in Ukraine, and humanized the system in line with restructuring in the nonmilitary educational sector.[28]

The question of loyalty to the newly independent state is also reflected in the gradual attempt to Ukrainianize the armed forces it inherited. At the very least, it would give the armed forces a Ukrainian "profile" as well as encourage those non-Ukrainians who took the oath of loyalty for nonpatriotic reasons to find other employment. By the end of 1995, instruction in the military academies was to take place exclusively in Ukrainian (a highly unlikely prospect). According to the directive, "knowledge of the Ukrainian language is an important means for the military and patriotic training of servicemen."[29]

Ukraine's military policies were possibly too successful. It inherited a bloated officer corps from the former Soviet armed forces, whose loyalty is difficult to gauge. But the policy did prevent the continued presence of Russian military bases on its territory, an important factor in the event of domestic strife and separatist revolts.

Dispute with Russia: Air Force

The main conflict with Russia regarding the ownership of air force equipment has involved the strategic bombers whose mission was to deliver ALCMs. This bomber force initially expressed strong reservations about taking the Ukrainian oath of loyalty. Since Ukraine successfully took control of the majority of the strategic bombers, it has been at a loss what to do with them, prompting Moscow to renew claims to them in spring 1993.

The elite airborne division at Bolgrad in the Western region of Odesa oblast, which had supplied weapons to Gagauz separatists in Moldova before December 1991, remained problematical until spring 1993. By summer 1992, 60 percent had taken the Russian oath and the remainder a Ukrainian oath of loyalty.[30] It could not undertake training operations, however, because its aircraft had been nationalized by Ukraine after the maintenance staff had completely defected to Kiev. In spring 1993 its remaining equipment was divided 50:50 between Russia and Ukraine, and those troops who had taken the Russian oath were transferred to the Russian Federation. This peaceful division of former Soviet military equipment contrasts with the stalemate surrounding the Black Sea Fleet because of its linkage to possession of the Crimea.

The dispute with Russia over the strategic bombers Ukraine inherited has largely evaporated. Unless Ukraine wants to utilize them for the delivery of ALCMs as a nuclear power, they will be irrelevant to its military requirements. Ukraine could sell or exchange them for energy supplies to Russia, but the fear that they could be then used against it in a future conflict may deter it from taking this decision.

Dispute with Russia: Black Sea Fleet

The Black Sea Fleet has been, and is likely to remain, a source of friction between Ukraine and Russia,[31] because it is connected to the Crimean question. The growing conflict in spring 1992 between Ukraine and Russia over the Black Sea Fleet was used by both sides to distract attention from domestic economic problems. Angry over price rises, President Yeltsin told industrial workers whom he was visiting in Ulyansk that "the Black Sea Fleet was, is and will be Russian. No one, not even Kiev, will take it away from Russia."[32] An agreement in mid-January 1992 that agreed to divide the fleet into "strategic" (CIS) and "conventional" (Ukrainian) sections was never carried out.

During the first quarter of 1992, the Ukrainian position increasingly radicalized from that of arguing in favor of only obtaining a section of the Black Sea Fleet to laying claim to all of the vessels and equipment on Ukrainian territory. As the Ukrainian position gradually hardened, Admiral Vladimir Chernavin, CIS navy commander, offered to increase Ukraine's share to 20 to 30 percent of the Black Sea Fleet (a figure later increased to 40 percent).[33] From spring 1992, after the tactical nuclear missiles were removed from the fleet, the "strategic" argument was replaced by more nationalistic, emotional, and historical arguments on the Russian side; they have continued to solidify since then into a coherent strategy.

Sevastopol was the scene of two of the most famous and heroic defenses in Russian history in the Crimean War and World

War II. Yet the actual military significance of the Black Sea Fleet has always been in doubt. The fighting history of the fleet ended in the 1853–1856 Crimean War; the fleet stood largely aloof from World War I developments and was scuttled by the Bolsheviks after the majority of ships raised the Ukrainian flag in 1918. Similarly in World War II, it played no role because the Black Sea was not a militarily significant region. It would be difficult today to construct a convincing military rationale on strategic grounds for the CIS or Russia to have a large fleet in the Black Sea, an area of dubious global or maritime importance. Defense of the principal shipping routes into the Mediterranean would be best served by shore-based maritime aircraft, which are plentiful.[34]

Consequently, initial claims by the CIS High Command that the Black Sea Fleet was required to counter the American Sixth Fleet or NATO in the Mediterranean Sea smacked more of traditional cold war rhetoric than any real basis in contemporary strategic thinking. In addition, the Black Sea Fleet is docked-up, owing to the lack of funds and fuel for training exercises, and is therefore both an easy target and a waste of resources as the condition and salability of the ships decline.

In contrast to the Baltic republics, where Russian commanders have admitted that the Baltic Fleet can no longer remain in (the now foreign ports of) Latvia and Estonia, there is a strongly held reluctance to admit the same situation exists for Sevastopol, which is now demanded as the home, after a possible division of the fleet, for the Russian Black Sea Fleet. The conflict over the Black Sea Fleet is thus entangled within the web of Russian-Ukrainian relations, Russian attitudes toward Ukrainian independence, and the issue of the possession of the Crimea.[35]

The urgency of finding a resolution to the Crimean question, after the declaration of independence in May 1992, followed the "war of decrees" between the presidents of Russia and Ukraine over the subordination of the Black Sea Fleet to Ukraine and the negotiations in Odesa that failed to find a solution to this question.[36] The Yalta agreement in August 1992 forced Ukraine to back down from its decree claiming all ships registered in

Ukrainian ports, but at the same time Russia conceded that it had to increase its previous 20 to 30 percent offer.[37]

In line with Ukraine's position that only the fleet, not land-based facilities, should be divided, former defense minister Morozov unilaterally went ahead and replaced land-based garrison commanders, including the Sevastopol garrison, with Ukrainians to the protest of local pro-Russian political groups and the Russian Ministry of Defense. In September 1992 all Black Sea Fleet land-based facilities were subordinated to Kiev, including naval academies in Sevastopol, the scene of bitter conflicts between cadets divided by the oaths–Russian or Ukrainian–they had taken.[38] On at least two occasions shots have been fired by naval patrols on training missions with Ukrainian air defense facilities near Sevastopol.[39] There would be great Ukrainian domestic opposition to transferring these land-based facilities to Russian jurisdiction, which President Kuchma will be obliged to take into account.

But Russian demands have continued to insist that "Sevastopol is, and will, be the Russian naval base," a view backed by Russian foreign minister Kozyrev.[40] Kozyrev argued that "the same relates to the Black Sea Fleet, whose division is absurd in itself. Sevastopol was Russia's naval base and it must remain as such." On a visit to Sevastopol in December 1994, Moscow Mayor Yuriy Luzhkov called it the "second perfecture of Moscow" and "Russia's outpost on its borders."[41]

The July 1993 summit between the Ukrainian and Russian presidents confirmed the 50:50 division of the fleet by 1995; but its ratification by either the Russian or Ukrainian parliaments was immediately thrown into doubt. The Russian parliament and Ministry of Defense supports a large body of opinion in the increasingly politicized officer corps of the fleet opposing its division, while many of these officers would probably also welcome the claim to Russian sovereignty over the city of Sevastopol and therefore could not accept any lease of this base because it would recognize Ukrainian sovereignty. President Yuriy Meshkov of the Crimean republic also supports a united fleet; his election has made the issue of resolving the fleet question even more difficult.

In September 1993, the Massandra summit raised the stakes when Russia demanded to be allowed to purchase the Ukrainian half of the fleet and land-based facilities. The Ukrainians agreed only to "consider" the demand. The parliamentary committee on legislation and legality reacted sharply to any suggestion of a lease that could only be decided by itself–and not the president. Second, it voiced the view of the bulk of the Ukrainian leadership that the transfer of the entire fleet and land-based facilities to Russia would "lead unavoidably to an aggravation of the political situation in Crimea and even to Crimea's secession from the composition of Ukraine."[42]

The agreements reached to date have tended to postpone decisions, attempting compromise only after claims, counterclaims, and crisis. Meanwhile, the officer corps within the fleet is becoming increasingly politicized, making compromise less likely. Although the majority of the officers within the fleet remain Russian, 80 percent of the conscripts are Ukrainian.[43] Therefore, any conflict within the Crimea could sharply divide the fleet along ethnic lines.

As the conflict ebbed and flowed during 1992–1994, the Ukrainian side should have come around to the view that it would have been better to demand that Russia take the entire fleet to its Novorossisk base and the Pacific and northern fleets, thereby leaving Sevastopol and the Crimea completely. This would certainly have forced the Russians to come clean–are they interested in the fleet or territorial acquisitions (or both)? To evict from Ukrainian territory those ships within the fleet that support Russia would be physically impossible–and highly provocative. Therefore, the best solution would be to sell or give the entire fleet to Russia with the proviso that it withdraw it from the Crimea to Russian or other CIS ports.

A solution to the Black Sea Fleet dispute still seems far away. Ukraine demanded that Ukraine and Russia draw up an inventory of Black Sea Fleet vessels as of 1991 before reaching a decision on future status. The Russian side is continuing to argue that the basis for negotiations are the Massandra accords, according to the Russian government's interdepartmental commission for the social affairs of service personnel. The underlying tensions within the Black Sea Fleet were brought to the service in April 1994 when Ukrainian special forces stormed a naval base in Odesa, arrested three officers, and then nationalized it after a fleet ship sailed to Sevastopol without Ukrainian authorization. A Russian diplomat described the Odesa incident as "the most large-scale and brazen anti-Russian action of all taken by the Ukrainian side."[44]

Both Ukraine and Russia demanded total control, then decided to divide it, with Russia finally again demanding it completely. Undoubtedly, President Yeltsin's tough line at the September 1993 Massandra summit was aimed to bolster his domestic nationalistic credentials, but in the process he also damaged former president Kravchuk's domestic standing. A solution to the Black Sea Fleet dispute will be difficult to find because the national interests of Russia and Ukraine are diametrically opposed in the Crimea. Although Yeltsin and Kuchma are unlikely to take their countries to war over the fleet or Crimea, the same cannot be said of others who aspire to sit in the presidential chair of Moscow or Kiev.

After the conflict in Odesa, Ukraine and Russia agreed again to divide the fleet at the Moscow CIS summit, with Ukraine taking 50 percent. According to Kravchuk, "Ukraine will take as much as it needs for its military and strategic needs" out of this sum and then sell the remainder. Reports suggest Ukraine would keep 15 to 20 percent of the amount it receives from the fleet for its own use (or 50 to 60 out of 300 vessels).

Of Ukraine's share, 30 to 35 percent would be sold to Russia in return for payment of its energy bills. Kravchuk's then military adviser, Major-General Volodymyr Petenko, estimated Ukraine's 50 percent share to be valued at $17 billion. It is quite possible that Russia would lease Sevastopol as its Black Sea Fleet base with the remaining shore infrastructure, including radar and hospitals, going to Ukraine. In anticipation, Ukraine has already begun establishing Fleet Base administrations in Izmail, Mykolayiv, and Ochakiv where, together with Odesa, Ukraine presumably would base its navy. It is still too early to say whether this agreement, in contrast to its four predecessors, will be implemented.[45] By early 1995, agreement on the Black Sea Fleet had still not been resolved, owing to Russia's persistent claims to a long-term lease (99 years) of the bulk of the Crimea's naval bases and exclusive control over the entire city of Sevastopol.

Nuclear Forces: Policies and Disputes

The West, START I, and Ratification

The START I treaty was signed by the United States and the USSR on July 31, 1991, but was not yet ratified before the disintegration of the USSR in December of that year. The issue of which states should become the "successor states" to the former Soviet nuclear commitments was only resolved on May 23, 1992, when the Lisbon Protocol designated all four republics of the former USSR with Strategic Nuclear Forces (Russia, Ukraine, Kazakhstan, and Belarus) as "successor states" to the former USSR for the purposes of START I.

The Lisbon Protocol called upon the three non-Russian states to accede to the Nuclear Non-Proliferation Treaty "in the shortest possible time." The Lisbon Protocol, an integral component of START I, and the NPT aimed to remove any newer nuclear weapons not perceived as being covered by START I in these republics (in the Ukrainian case, newer 46 SS-24 missiles and ALCMs). Ukraine had persistently argued since late 1991 for a place at the nuclear negotiation table (which the Lisbon Protocol gave it), hoping to use it to bolster Ukraine's international reputation as well as confirm Western legitimacy on Ukraine's equal standing with Russia.

Before signing START I and the Lisbon Protocol, former president Kravchuk sent a letter to former president Bush in which he qualified his promises to eliminate nuclear weapons within the seven-year deadline.[46] First, this process would be undertaken "taking into account the national security interests" of Ukraine. Second, dismantling of Ukrainian nuclear weapons would have to ensure that no other country (principally Russia) could "reuse" them.

Ukrainians initially misinterpreted the ratification process and attempted to divide START I and the Lisbon Protocol from the NPT (yet the Lisbon Protocol is what gives Ukraine a relationship to START I in the first place). First, Ukrainians were mistaken in their belief that START I and the Lisbon Protocol were separate documents: the Lisbon Protocol is an integral legal component of START I. Second, Kiev was mistaken in believing that the older SS-19 missiles can be divorced from the newer SS-24s and ALCMs. The START I treaty does not only cover SS-19 nuclear missiles, and the five nuclear powers will not accept a definition of it in such terms. Finally, for the purposes of international law, Kravchuk's signature to START I and the Lisbon Protocol means that he is legally bound not to do anything in contradiction of them.

Dispute with Russia: Nuclear Weapons

Ukraine's ambivalent and increasingly pro-nuclear stance contributed to worsening relations with Russia. Russia could launch a preemptive military strike to take control of or disable nuclear weapons in Ukraine if it feared that Kiev was close to obtaining positive control.

It is highly unlikely that President Yeltsin discussed "the possibility of a nuclear exchange between the independent Ukraine and Russia" with senior military officers in October 1992. Yeltsin and Gorbachev's suggestion that Ukrainian leaders "read too many newspapers" did little to assuage the deeply held suspicions and mistrust felt by Ukraine toward Russia.[47] Similarly, remarks made by the "shadow foreign minister" of the National Salvation Front were replayed in Ukrainian newspapers without any condemnation from President Yeltsin: "The situation with Ukraine is growing ever more dangerous and, we as professionals, should study the possible scenario of an unexpected nuclear war with Kiev, which, should it break out, will be conducted without the rules produced by geopolitical thinking during the period of (nuclear) parity."[48] Such comments have only served to convince

Ukrainian leaders that after they denuclearized Russia would use nuclear blackmail against them.

Senior Russian leaders have threatened on many occasions that they could not allow Ukraine to remain a nuclear power. Possession of nuclear weapons would contribute to worsening Russian-Ukrainian relations, thereby sharpening Ukrainian security fears, distracting financial resources from other more important areas that would be better served in bolstering Ukrainian security.

Ownership

In February 1993 Ukraine called for the drawing up of a special protocol to START to define the issue of ownership. The CIS heads of state attempted to unsuccessfully clarify this problem on a number of occasions, especially at Bishkek. The United States, together with Russia and the CIS Joint Armed Forces High Command, consistently argued since December 1991 that all nuclear weapons in the former USSR are the property of Russia. Until September 1992 nuclear weapons in all four republics were under the control of the CIS when Russia demanded they should come under its direct control—and Ukraine refused.[49]

It is not clear whether this was the catalyst or events were themselves already moving toward Ukraine's rejection of this Russian move and de facto nationalization of all former Soviet assets on its territory.[50] What is clear is that, although the Ukrainian November 1992 declaration laying claim to ownership of strategic nuclear weapons followed the transfer of CIS to Russian control over nuclear forces, nevertheless it merely followed the logic of events already instituted since April of the same year in Ukraine. The only difference was that Kiev itself began to fully finance the strategic nuclear bases from November 1992. Ukraine is unlikely to change its position on this question; to do so would require recognizing the Russian strategic nuclear bases on its territory, which would be anathema to the Ukrainian leadership.

Undoubtedly two factors played a part in Ukraine's move to take de facto control over nuclear weapons on its territory. First, it prevented Russian ownership and control over the bases and represented a step toward becoming a permanent nuclear power, for those who desired this status. Second, Ukraine had received no compensation when tactical nuclear missiles were transferred to Russia by May 1992 and when Russia nationalized all former Soviet assets in Moscow and abroad (Ukraine had persistently demanded a share equal to the sum it would pay as its share of former Soviet liabilities). De facto control would ensure Ukraine some compensation for the strategic nuclear weapons remaining on Ukrainian territory.

The Russia-U.S. agreement announced on August 31, 1992, allowed the United States to purchase enriched uranium over 10 years at a cost of $5 billion to $10 billion, merely reinforcing Kiev's view that it was being squeezed out. But the United States did later consent not to sign any agreement until an accord between Russia and Ukraine had been arrived at on dividing the proceeds–nearly $13 billion over 10 years–for upwards of 500 tons of highly enriched uranium.[51]

Ukrainian Policies

There were no legal constraints on Ukraine to join the NPT regime before all nuclear weapons are removed from its territory. But the argument that increasingly gained the upper hand in Kiev was that Ukraine should ratify START I and the Lisbon Protocol, believing that it covers only 36 percent of nuclear weapons in Ukraine (or 50 older, Russian-built SS-19 missiles). Pavlychko, former head of the parliamentary committee on foreign affairs, believed that the Ukrainian parliament would ratify START I in September or October 1993 and the NPT in 1995, when the entire treaty came up for review.[52] On many occasions, various Ukrainian leaders, including former president Kravchuk, argued that the fate of the 46 SS-24 missiles would have to be settled by separate agreement between Ukraine, Russia, and the United States (in Ukrainian eyes they were not covered by the September 1993 Massandra summit).[53]

In other words, the nuclear disarmament process would be dragged out over a period longer than the seven years allowed under START I (and especially over the three years provided by

CIS agreements). The SS-24 missiles and ALCMs would act as an "insurance policy" while Ukraine is building its economy, armed forces, and national identity during a period when a nationalistic and irredentist Russian president could come to power.[54]

In summer 1993 and March 1994 at Pervomaysk, Ukraine did begin to unilaterally disband a regiment of 10 SS-19 missiles with 60 warheads. Two factors pushed the Ukrainians to begin dismantling these missiles. First, the missiles were targeted at the United States. Their dismantling occurred on the eve of former defense minister Morozov's visit to the United States in July 1993 and President Kravchuk's visit to the United States in March 1994; hence the dismantlings were acts of good faith intended to repair relations between Kiev and Washington. The Morozov visit led to the signing of a memorandum to "promote confidence and enhance understanding between the defense and military establishments."[55]

Second, the missiles had come to the end of their warranty and service life on combat duty. Keeping them in service would have incurred a large expenditure and would have been potentially dangerous.[56] The dismantling of the nuclear missiles was undertaken without parliamentary approval, a surprising move that reflects the relative indifference toward the fate of SS-19 missiles within the Ukrainian leadership.

Other factors that play a prominent role within this pronuclear lobby are symbolic and psychological—for example, the use of nuclear weapons to bolster self-confidence and equality with Russia during a transitional period. Nuclear weapons in the former USSR symbolized prestige and grandeur and represented the independence and dignity of the state. It would be surprising if none of these factors had rubbed off on the Ukrainian political elite, who were all brought up as *Homos Sovieticus*. In these cases, the question of whether Ukraine has operational control is irrelevant: "It is like having a gun displayed on your wall. It may have no bullets, but when your neighbor comes to dinner he is afraid of it," Pavlychko argued.[57] Ukraine will feel psychologically vulnerable to greater Russian pressure once all of the nuclear weapons are removed from its territory.

Upon returning from the United States in January 1993,

deputy foreign minister Tarasiuk was exposed to strong criticism for the "vague and ineffectual guaranties" with which he had returned (in May of the same year Tarasiuk himself said that these "guaranties" were "insufficient"). As relations continued to deteriorate with Russia, Kiev expanded the definition of "security guarantees" to include nuclear and conventional attacks, economic and political pressure, as well as territorial integrity and the inviolability of its borders.[58]

Of these, external economic and political pressure are the most likely scenarios, yet impossible to quantify or give "guarantees" against. The security guarantees should go even as far as to ensure, in Tarasiuk's eyes, that Ukraine would *never* be the object of aggression or economic-political pressure.[59] Tarasiuk has also since added, confirming Ukraine's position as a "moving target," that the security guarantees should ensure the inspection and monitoring of denuclearization in Russia.[60] During 1993–1994, although Ukrainian leaders talked of security "guarantees," the West talked only of security "assurances," which were in fact granted in December 1994.

An additional complication has been compensation. The United States looked at the Ukrainian nuclear question from the viewpoint of just paying the costs of nuclear disarmament, and hence only offered the sum of $175 million to Ukraine. Kiev, meanwhile, looked at this question from many angles, including the costs of dismantlement; the social costs of reemploying and relocating redundant Strategic Rocket Troops and employees in the military industrial complex; the costs to cover potential environmental damage, economic aid, compensation to cover Ukraine's contribution to the Soviet nuclear buildup; and, finally, an "inducement" sufficiently large to entice Ukraine to move in its stated direction of becoming a non-nuclear power. In the words of former deputy premier Ihor Yukhnovsky, "Ukraine should benefit from its non-nuclear status."

Ukraine initially demanded $1.5 billion for nuclear disarmament (the total Nunn-Lugar appropriation is only $800 million). This was later described as only a "preliminary assessment" by the Ukrainian Foreign Ministry, blaming its upward revision to $2–3 billion upon Russia's insistence that it pay world prices for oil and gas. The "preliminary assessment," however, was not backed by any published analysis of the costs.[61] It was certainly the case that Ukraine was using world, not Ukrainian, prices while the great variety of figures suggests that the majority of them were merely plucked from thin air.[62] Former president Kravchuk, meanwhile, believed that the total value of the fissionable material in the warheads in Ukraine was as high as $6 billion.

Administrative and Operational Control[63]

In April 1992, Ukraine instituted a policy of administrative control over strategic nuclear bases. It covers all aspects of the nuclear weapons except the ability to launch them, but allegedly includes the ability to block their firing by Russia. Thus, Ukraine has "negative control" over the nuclear weapons on its territory, which could be the first step toward becoming a full nuclear power.

On April 5, 1992, a secret Ministry of Defense decree placed all military forces in Ukraine under Kiev's control, including Strategic Rocket Troops. Administrative control ensured Ukrainian control over all personnel, finances, logistics, supplies, Strategic Rocket Troop appointments by Kiev, and Strategic Rocket Troop oaths of loyalty to Ukraine in the strategic nuclear bases in Ukraine. A "Centre for the Administrative Command and Control of Troops of the Strategic Nuclear Forces" was created within the Ukrainian Ministry of Defense. The April 1992 secret decree was followed by instructions to the Cabinet of Ministers to immediately investigate the means "to ensure active technical control by Ukraine" to prevent non-use by Russia of nuclear missiles located in Ukraine. This was followed by instructions to the Ministry of Defense to ensure that the Strategic Rocket Troops be complimented henceforth by Ukrainian conscripts and officers who would take the Ukrainian oath.[64] Only Ukrainian conscripts and officers in the Strategic Rocket Troops, who have been required to take the Ukrainian oath since summer 1992, have been employed.

Another aspect of this negative control has been Kiev's claim that it can block the launch of nuclear missiles fired by Moscow from its territory. Initially, Kravchuk claimed that former CIS commander-in-chief Evgenii Shaposhnikov promised all three non-Russian republics with strategic nuclear weapons the means to be able to block the firing of nuclear weapons by Russia, but this was never forthcoming. Although there is no question that Ukraine has worked on the means to block the missiles since April 1992, it is not clear whether Kravchuk was bluffing when he claimed in December 1992 that he possessed the means to undertake this or whether the ability to block launch merely rests on Ukrainian control and loyalty of the Strategic Rocket Troops.

In December 1992, for example, Kravchuk claimed that he was capable of ordering Strategic Rocket Troops to "prepare special signals, which enable the blocking of the firing intercontinental ballistic rockets when the order for their release is not in agreement with the president of Ukraine. With this in mind there is a direct contact to the commanders of Strategic Rocket Forces on Ukrainian territory."[65] Four months later Kravchuk admitted that the blocking of unauthorized launch was not a technical-mechanical method, "but by an order, a directive" by telephone to the Strategic Rocket Troops.[66] He could have been simply bluffing.

Moscow claimed in spring 1993 that Ukraine was attempting to retarget and break the PAL security system, which is required in order to retarget the missiles. U.S. intelligence estimated that Ukraine would take 12 to 18 months to obtain positive control (Russia estimated only 6 to 9 months). To disarm the PALs requires removing the warheads and installing new arming devices that are controlled by Kiev. Ukraine was a manufacturer of PALs at the secret *Monolith* factory and thus has the experience to break the codes and replace them with Kiev-controlled ones. Speculation has surfaced, however, that the warheads are equipped with a permanent disabling device if incorrect PAL codes are entered (although only 45 to 65 percent of former Soviet nuclear weapons are estimated to have PALs).[67]

Yet obtaining operational control over nuclear weapons would not give Ukraine the complete nuclear infrastructure required to be a full-fledged nuclear power. The technical infrastructure necessary for "strategic stability" includes early warning systems, communications centers, attack assessment, and survival control. Ukraine would require the geodetic wording of targets and assistance guidance software—which only Russia possesses.[68]

Finally, Ukraine's military industrial complex lacks the ability to produce some components required for servicing nuclear missiles.

Ukrainian administrative control over nuclear bases was strengthened in the winter of 1993–1994.[69] On January 21, 1994 (only one week after the Trilateral statement), the commander of the 43rd Missile Army Strategic Rocket Troops in Ukraine, Lieutenant General Vladimir Mikhtiuk, took the Ukrainian oath of loyalty. Mikhtiuk was then promoted by Kravchuk to the rank of colonel-general. All SRT servicemen are reportedly being forced to take the Ukrainian oath, although every second officer is striving to be transferred to Russia.

Two out of three top SRT commanders in Ukraine took the oath (Mikhtiuk and Major-General N. Filatov), together with 1,400 out of 2,300 officers. Major-General R. Karimov, who refused to take the oath, was unilaterally replaced by Colonel Volodymyr Shvets as commander of the 19th missile division. The SRT officer level is therefore at only 50 to 60 percent strength, according to Russian military sources. Undoubtedly the Ukrainian leadership, which highly distrusts Russia, wants to ensure complete control over the implementation of its own denuclearization. Possibly, it could also be an extra insurance policy if Ukraine decided to become a nuclear power after all, in response to future negative developments within Russia.

Trilateral Nuclear Statement

After the collapse of the September 1993 Massandra accords between Russia and Ukraine, stalemate continued as Kiev dragged out the ratification of START I and the NPT. The Ukrainian parliament did go some way toward dealing with this question on November 18, 1993, when it ratified START I, but only with a large number of reservations primarily dealing with security and financial factors.

Why did Kravchuk move in January of the following year to force the issue into the lap of the Ukrainian parliament?[70] He could have reasoned that his popularity was now so low (10 to 15 percent) that it would not affect his domestic standing. Second, he has always been a politician in the Gorbachevian mold–

more interested in, and more capable of, playing the role of international statesman than cajoling a conservative legislature into adopting economic reforms. Third, the November 1993 ratification of START I with reservations had laid the basis for a negotiated compromise to Ukraine's nuclear dilemma, which the United States could broker.

Past evidence of attempted agreements between Russia and Ukraine during the last two years had shown their futility and inability to reach a mutually acceptable compromise. On this occasion the United States stepped in as honest broker. Growing regionalism in the Donbas and separatism in Crimea (coupled with an economic and energy crisis) made the Ukrainian parliament more amenable to compromise. Finally, by the end of 1993, there was growing concern at Ukraine's international isolation, which, if left to continue, could have swelled the core pronuclear lobby and bolstered a more uncompromising nationalistic Ukrainian position.

The trilateral statement between the three countries on January 14, 1994, was initially sharply attacked by parliamentarians. Former parliamentary chairman Pliushch claimed, "I cannot see the observances of Ukraine's economic interests nor guarantees for Ukrainian security, so much spoken about in the Moscow document." He continued: "What happened in Moscow is not nuclear disarmament, but stripping the state naked in military, economic and political terms."[71]

On February 4, 1994, the Ukrainian parliament voted overwhelmingly in favor of dropping the reservations it had originally added in November of the previous year and ratified START I and the Lisbon Protocol.[72] Of 450 deputies, only 292 were in the hall; 260 of them voted in favor of full ratification (3 against and 29 abstained). The vote came after Kravchuk warned of the dangers of international isolation and the aging of the warheads. It was coupled with an announcement that the United States would double U.S. aid to Ukraine to $700 million (half of which was scheduled for nuclear disarmament).

The Ukrainian parliamentary resolution welcomed the readiness of the United States and Russia to provide "security guarantees" to Ukraine after it joined START and the NPT. In addition, the resolution would "take into consideration obligations taken by the United States, Russian Federation and the U.K. regarding Ukraine to respect its independence, sovereignty and existing borders, avoid the threat of the use of force or use of force against Ukrainian territorial integrity or political independence, avoid economic pressure and obligations not to use this as a weapon against Ukraine." The resolution also welcomed additional compensation and Ukrainian military control "over the dismantling and extraction of strategic nuclear warheads on the territory of Russia."

The full ratification of START I and the Lisbon Protocol failed to deal with a number of issues. These included Ukraine's accession to the NPT, Ukraine's demand that it be compensated for tactical nuclear weapons withdrawn to Russia between February and May 1992, and definition of the exact meaning of the term "security guarantees" (in Ukrainian eyes) or "security assurances" (in the West's eyes). Other outstanding issues include the final disposition of the silos (which Ukraine would like not to destroy), timetable for implementing denuclearization and continuous supplies of Russian energy (enriched uranium, oil, and gas).[73]

Continued progress in U.S.-Ukrainian relations, which have appreciably warmed since December 1993 while U.S. relations with Russia have declined, depends on continued Ukrainian denuclearization and implementation of economic reform, both of which Kiev was reluctant to undertake under Kravchuk. Implementation of Ukraine's denuclearization still therefore faces many obstacles and dangers.

Ukraine's relations with the United States continued to improve in the second half of 1994. The United States approved further financial aid of $200 million during President Kuchma's visit to the United States in November, bringing total aid to $900 million over 1994–1995. Increased financial aid and political support from the United States was in gratitude for President Kuchma's support for reform and ratification of the NPT, both of which he persuaded parliament to endorse.[74] The UK, United States, and the Russian Federation signed a joint declaration spelling out security assurances to Ukraine in exchange for its ratification of the NPT. The assurances "respect the independence and sovereignty and the existing borders of Ukraine," "refrain from the threat or use of force against the territorial integrity or political independence," and "refrain from economic coercion." The assurances also commit the signatories to provide assistance to Ukraine if it is attacked and "will consult in the event a situation arises which raises a question concerning these commitments."[75]

Conclusion

Ukraine inherited a large volume of military equipment and military units that are deployed away from Kiev's main security threat and are, to some extent, deteriorating from lack of maintenance, spare parts, and fuel. Nevertheless, they should be of sufficient size and quality to prevent any external threats from becoming a serious concern in the near future. Even after the CFE treaty limits are implemented, Ukraine will still have large numbers of equipment and troops. The major military threat to Ukrainian territorial integrity lies in eastern-southern Ukraine and the Crimea, a factor that will discourage leasing Sevastopol to Russia.

Ukraine succeeded in peacefully nationalizing the three-fourths million former Soviet armed forces on its territory. But the loyalty of the non-Ukrainian officer ranks contributes to Ukrainian insecurity. The scarcity of resources and competition for housing amidst economic crisis and conflict with Russia is likely to lead to preferences being given to those officers considered loyal to Kiev, as the armed forces are reduced in size. This will lead to resentment among those officers who are accused of being disloyal and who, after all, took the Ukrainian oath of loyalty.

The question of the Black Sea Fleet is a lingering source of tension between Russia and Ukraine and an important source of Ukrainian insecurity. U.S. offers of mediation between Ukraine and Russia should be accepted on this question. Five agreements reached between Ukraine and Russia during 1992–1994 have failed to resolve the Black Sea fleet question. In addition, tying the fleet's status to that of the city of Sevastopol, and indirectly the Crimea, by the Russian Ministry of Defense and parliament is tantamount to Russia's holding a territorial claim on Ukrainian territory.

U.S. efforts at mediation would be best served by removing this conflict, which not only clouds Ukrainian-Russian relations but also influences Kiev's attitudes toward nuclear weapons. The fleet could either be rapidly divided, and the Russian portion removed to other ports and fleets based on its territory, or the Ukrainians could be encouraged to give away the bulk of the fleet in return for which it would be asked to vacate Ukrainian ports. The removal of the Black Sea Fleet to Russian territory could be undertaken during the denuclearization period, thereby resolving two deep-seated conflicts that contribute to Ukrainian insecurity.

Despite the Trilateral Statement of January 1994 and Ukrainian ratification of START I, Ukrainian denuclearization still depends on many questions outside its control. The key element—implementation—still lies ahead. Kravchuk was initially unwilling to cajole parliament to ratify the documents he himself had demanded Ukraine be allowed to join (START I and NPT) as well as the ones he himself signed in May 1992. Primarily he feared losing popularity or being accused of harboring "unpatriotic" credentials.

At the same time, the West's failure to look at Ukraine's nuclear weapons in any context other than proliferation has neglected the security dimension of the domestic debate in Kiev. After all, the only way the West could encourage Ukraine to realize that nuclear weapons would not increase its security is by discussing its security fears. If, as was the case for nearly two years, these security fears were ignored, together with the complicated psychological-historical context of Ukrainian-Russian relations, the impasse between the positions of both sides (the United States and Ukraine) would widen, allowing the pronuclear lobby to grow alongside Kiev's deep-seated insecurity.

Yet Western nuclear powers will not give Ukraine binding security guarantees (in contrast to security assurances), particularly against external unquantifiable economic/political pressures (but these are a more likely "threat" than nuclear or conventional attacks). Ukraine's demand for security guarantees were not met. It is unlikely that U.S. or NATO forces would defend Ukrainian territorial integrity although this is what a guarantee implies.

The ratification of the START I treaty by Ukraine in February left only the NPT outstanding, a major obstacle to improving Ukraine's relations with the West, from whence the bulk of the aid would be found to support Ukrainian reforms. On the eve of President Kuchma's visit to the United States in November 1994, the Ukrainian parliament voted to ratify the NPT, although still claiming that it "owned" the nuclear weapons on its territory. This, in turn, released security assurances by the major nuclear powers to Ukraine (although not security guarantees that Kiev had long demanded).

Ukraine inherited formidable military elements with which to implement a national security policy if and when one is formulated. Despite an entire range of problems (deployment, budget, officer loyalty, et cetera), Ukraine has sufficiently large armed and security forces to defend its security interests. Obstacles to resolving the Black Sea Fleet dispute are formidable; its link to the Crimean question is regarded as indisputable throughout the Russian leadership, and the positions of both Ukraine and Russia are hardening after an initial period of compromise. These questions are therefore likely to heat up dangerously in 1995–1996, when the next presidential and parliamentary elections will be held in Russia.

What are the keys to ensuring that Ukraine's security environment is not perceived as unfriendly? The West must contribute in mediating Russian-Ukrainian relations and creating a new security architecture in central-eastern Europe; Ukraine must overcome its domestic political and economic crisis; and Ukrainian-Russian relations must improve. Unless these factors are addressed, Ukrainian insecurity will remain profound, thereby impeding Ukraine's commitment to achieving non-nuclear status and stability in the region.

5

Conclusion

Trends

Legacy of External Domination and Totalitarianism

Ukraine's legacy differs in two crucial ways from that of the former colonies of the Western powers. First, Ukraine inherited hundreds of years of external domination by various powers over its many regions; its territories were reunited into one state only after World War II. Second, Ukraine also inherited more than seven decades of Soviet totalitarianism, in contrast to the British democracy received by India and other former British colonies.[1]

The devastating effects of Russian and Soviet nationality policies and repression created a desire within the Ukrainian leadership to give highest priority to establishing the Ukrainian state. This, coupled, with the legacy of the failure to establish an independent state on previous occasions, led to an emphasis on state-building measures, armed forces, and national security. In the light of Ukraine's historical legacy of external domination and Russian territorial claims, these steps may have been justified. Nevertheless, the Ukrainian leadership sorely neglected political and economic reform, thereby allowing the country to drift into stagnation during 1993–1994.

The different orientations of Ukraine's leaders and political parties, particularly vis-à-vis relations with Russia, growing regionalism, and disillusionment with the West, make it hard for Ukraine to clearly define its national interests and formulate a national security policy. Ukraine's lack of unifying factors – religion, nationalism, economic progress, and political reform – increase the difficulty. Given its history, Ukraine is highly likely to remain a status quo power in central-eastern Europe and to be fearful of border claims and changes. Any demands for basing rights or territorial revisions would be strongly opposed domestically out of the fear of unleashing a "domino" effect.

The legacy of Soviet totalitarianism and denationalization has dramatically affected the Ukrainian elite, programs of political parties, and the reform process. The weakness of the nationalist movement in December 1991 forced it to adopt an uneasy alliance with its former opponents – the national communists led by Kravchuk. This alliance ensured a high rate of support for independence and ethnic stability in 1992-1993.

Domestic Threats to Security

By mid-1993, the growing political and economic crisis first reflected itself in social unrest. It began in the russified Donbas region and led to the growth of trade union activism and, for the first time, an alliance between noncommunist groups and workers' movements. Second, the honeymoon ended between nationalists and national communists over the twin questions of Economic Union with Russia and the Massandra summit of Russian and Ukrainian presidents. Finally, growing political activism forced early parliamentary and presidential elections to occur in 1994.

Symptomatic of the deepening political and economic crisis were the growth of regionalism and the demands for autonomy, even separatism. The major asset of the national communists in December 1991 had been their influence throughout Ukraine; they had been able to organize support for the newly independent state in areas where the nationalists were either weak or nonexistent. But by mid-1993, the unconstituted "party of power" was itself divided between pro- and anti-Russian orientations, with the latter particularly influential in the Donbas and insistent on the need for economic union with Russia.[2]

The short honeymoon between nationalists and national communists was costly. Stability was translated into missed opportunities to push for change during the first half of 1992. Hyperinflation occurred, corruption rose, and organized crime increased; yet Ukraine had no reform program. Kravchuk was unable, or unwilling, to steer the country in a clear direction.

The growing economic crisis strengthened the calls of those who argued that the main cause lies in "broken ties" with Russia and hence the need for reintegration in an Economic Union. But this argument misses the main point—namely, that the root causes of the crisis lie in gross mismanagement, hyperinflationary monetary policy, and the lack of reform or privatization. After all, those who steadfastly support military, political, and economic union with Russia are traditionally anti-reform and oppose any transition to a market economy (Party of Labour, Party of Slavic Unity, Communist and Socialist groups). Hence, communists and socialists voted for Kuchma in the second round of the presidential elections because of his pro-Russian/CIS orientation.

Although it is not surprising to find nationalists opposed to the Economic Union, even moderates (such as Lanovyi) and the representatives of the new private business class argue against it. Kravchuk's compromise—associate membership in the Economic Union, so as not to "split Ukraine"—led to the usual failure to implement the agreement and to Ukraine's further muddling through. Current president Kuchma favors Ukraine's full membership in the CIS Economic Union. But unlike the communists, he will be cautiously disposed toward political-military integration, given the domestic hostility from nationalists and the security forces.

Kravchuk's drift toward support for the Economic Union reflected his continued disinterest in, or ideological hostility toward, economic reform, as well as his reliance upon antireform personnel within the government apparatus since October 1990. It can be no coincidence, therefore, that in summer 1993 Kravchuk offered to hold a referendum on whether Ukraine should build a socialist or capitalist economy, which was followed by the Kuchma government's proposals to return to centralized state planning. Former premier Kuchma's resignation speech to the Ukrainian parliament lamented that "anarchy has become the basic symptom of our economy as a result of the spontaneous and senseless collapse of the command mechanism. . . . " Clearly, the Ukrainian leadership had still to come to terms with the root causes of the economic crisis and its disastrous impact upon Ukrainian security.

The growing political and economic crisis brought into question the legitimacy of the newly independent state and the foundations upon which it was built. All of the structures of power in Ukraine became illegitimate and highly unpopular (presidency, government, and parliament), producing a potentially dangerous situation. The growing demands by even moderate, democratic groups to begin organizing paramilitary groups for two purposes—to meet crisis situations and threats to territorial integrity—were a dangerous symptom of the current under way within Ukraine, a current to which the former presidential and parliamentary leadership seemed oblivious.

If either the threat to territorial integrity or the domestic crisis continues to deepen, the role of the security forces will grow. Concern at the loyalty of the bloated officer corps, demands for officer ethnic cleansing, competition for scarce resources, and the need to reduce the armed forces are likely to place great strains on the Ukrainian leadership. If Ukrainian security fears remain high, or grow, these strains will worsen. The past experience of other countries (Argentina, Brazil, and Mexico) with hyperinflation and economic crisis points to the ability of authoritarian regimes to ultimately stabilize the situation and the tendency of democratic regimes to reflate the economy when faced by the competing demands of different interest groups. Not surprisingly, therefore, the trend toward support for an authoritarian solution is growing in Ukraine, supported to some degree by President Kuchma in his calls for strong executive power.

In 1993–1994, Kravchuk lost his power base in eastern-southern Ukraine, where he received a low number of votes in the summer 1994 presidential elections. His centrist approach to political and economic affairs may have been useful in early 1992, but by 1994 it merely perpetuated the lack of any clear direction and policy. Ukraine's new president will have to combine the centrist virtues of compromise and balance, which Ukraine needs to avoid being pulled in a nationalistic or pro-Russian direction, with a clearly articulated vision of a Western-leaning Ukraine committed to reform. Any Ukrainian president should possess three virtues—strong, decisive leadership, patriotism, and commitment to reform.

Finally, if the threat to Ukrainian territorial integrity becomes acute, particularly in areas where nationalist groups are weak, such as the Donbas or Crimean republic, nationalists may be tempted to again work a deal with those national communists who have an anti-Russian orientation. The price of such an alliance will be again high, especially over economic reform and hyperinflation.

The solution to reducing the danger of the growth of demands for autonomy and even separatism is to deal with the symptoms of the economic crisis. In addition, the key to reducing the danger of separatism is to improve relations with Russia, maintain membership in the CIS, and dampen anti-Russian rhetoric. These are all tall orders for Ukraine's new parliament and president.

The national communists, including Kravchuk, were better placed to negotiate with Moscow, avoid inflaming Russian sensitivities, and keep at bay Russian support for separatism. In a country where such a sharp division exists between those who look to Russia as their "best friend" or "worst enemy," the formulation of a security policy will be complicated and difficult even for Ukraine's post-Kravchuk leadership, which would like to mend fences with Moscow.

External Threats to Security

Only good relations with Russia would keep security issues from dominating the agenda of the Ukrainian elite. Improved relations would profoundly affect the degree of commitment and will be needed to achieve political and economic reform.

Although the Russian Foreign Ministry may be trying to garner United Nations support for its "peacekeeping" roles in the former USSR, there is strong evidence that the Russian military has inflamed conflicts in order to put pressure on republics to join the CIS and then base Russian "peacekeeping forces."[3] This trend in Russian relations with the former USSR is dangerous and likely to lead to instability and a worsening of relations with Ukraine; even Kuchma as premier complained of Russian economic pressure. The tough negotiating position of the Russian delegation at the September 1993 Massandra and April 1994 Crimean summits was dictated by the Ministry of Defence, which reiterated that it would never allow Ukraine to become a full nuclear power and that Sevastopol would be the future base of the Russian Black Sea Fleet. Russian demands in the Crimea have prevented the finalization of an agreement to deal with the Black Sea Fleet.

The range of issues that have contributed to the cold war between Ukraine and Russia make it unlikely that relations will quickly improve; if anything they are likely to worsen before they normalize. Russia will continue to possess a powerful leverage — energy supplies — for the foreseeable future, which will continue to contribute to Ukrainian vulnerabilities and insecurity. This, in turn, means increasing Ukraine's reliance upon the poorly designed and potentially dangerous Chornobyl-type nuclear power stations. The key again is to overcome the economic crisis in order to be able to purchase energy at world prices from other non-Russian sources, which is not an impossible task to accomplish (the Baltic republics' energy needs are met nearly 100 percent by Russia; in contrast Ukraine supplies 50 percent of its requirements).

Russian-Ukrainian relations will also continue to deteriorate because of the ethnic Chornobyl potentially awaiting the Crimea. Russian views of the Crimea influence and cloud Russian-Ukrainian relations, overshadowing other areas. There are growing calls for Sevastopol to be recognized as a Russian city with special federal status in the new Russian constitution. These calls greatly dissuade the Ukrainian leadership from agreeing to lease the city to the Russian navy, a demand with a wide basis of support in Russia. The Black Sea Fleet has no strategic value, but is being used merely as a front to maintain a foothold in the Crimea—the real prize. Two years of attempted compromise over ownership of the fleet have only ended up in stalemate. President Kuchma will have to tread carefully to avoid giving away too much for fear of a nationalist and military backlash. As time slips away a settlement looks even less likely.

The Crimean republic, with its large Ukrainian and Russian military and naval bases, the subject of which is broached by either Russian emotion or Ukrainian territorial insecurity, coupled with a Bosnian-style mix of different ethnic groups and orientations, has the dangerous potential of a new "Abkhazia" that could suck Russia and Ukraine into full-blown conflict. As Kravchuk predicted, "If we cannot resolve the issue of Sevastopol and the Crimea today, then the generations which follow us will settle it anyway, but with considerable bloodshed."

Russian and Ukrainian national interests are likely to increasingly diverge as the moderate, centrist approach is replaced by a nationalistic Russian leadership less willing to compromise. This clash of national interests is likely to occur in Moldova, Transcaucasus, the Balkans, and the Black Sea region. Both Georgia and Moldova have requested Ukrainian military aid and involvement against their respective Russian-backed secessionist rebellions. Ukraine has admitted to sending repaired tanks to Azerbaijan while Ukrainian right-wing paramilitaries have gained widespread popularity through their "struggle against Russian imperialism" in Abkhazia and Chechnya. Ukraine and Russia also have different interests vis-à-vis Moldova. Continued Russian support for Dniester Republican and Gagauz separatism within Moldova could drive the rump Moldova into reunification with Romania, a prospect that disturbs Ukraine and is likely to give impulse to further nationalistic tendencies and territorial claims from Romania.[4]

Although Ukraine ratified START I and the NPT in 1994, denuclearization will not be rushed. Instead there will be a preference for holding on to some nuclear weapons, as an "insurance policy" vis-à-vis Russia and to obtain continued Western aid. This will inevitably contribute to the further deterioration in relations with Russia that looks likely in other areas. The head of the Main Directorate for Nuclear Munitions, Colonel General Evhen Maslin, already claims that Ukraine has "full control" over nuclear weapons, while the strategic bomber and warhead maintenance crews have taken the Ukrainian oath. More disturbingly, he claimed that Ukraine could create systems that would allow it to attain launch capability within one to two years.[5] The possibility of Ukrainian military policy drifting in this direction is fraught with danger and could precipitate the very crisis in relations with Russia that Ukraine wishes to avoid.

Implications

The West

During 1992–1993, Ukraine's relations with the West were strained and by the end of 1993 had severely deteriorated. This study points to the various causes of this deterioration. The West was unable and unwilling to widen its relations beyond nuclear weapons or deepen them with Ukraine. It ignored Ukrainian security concerns and seemed unable to understand the deep insecurity of Ukraine's leadership. The West was also willing to ignore the negative trends in Russian security policy, particularly imperialistic tendencies toward the former USSR.

The new U.S. administration did attempt to mend fences with Ukraine in mid-1993, but this new policy did not bear fruit until the winter of 1993–1994, when a variety of breakthroughs occurred. Without the United States, it is unlikely Ukraine could have been coaxed into fully ratifying START I. Similar U.S. efforts at mediation should be applied to other burning Russian-Ukrainian areas of conflict, such as the Black Sea Fleet and Crimea. The current Russian president and government are adopting a cautious approach toward these questions for fear of derailing Ukraine's commitment to denuclearization. Nevertheless, the West should take into account Kiev's security fears after a nuclear-free

Ukraine faces a post-Yeltsin Russia that is likely to be nationalistic.

Whereas the question of compensation and aid could be overcome by good will on both the U.S. and Ukrainian sides, the United States will not provide the kind of steadfast guarantees that Ukraine has been demanding and that have consistently expanded over time. William Perry, U.S. secretary of defense, stated on a visit to Ukraine in March 1994 that the United States had not given security guarantees to any country during the last 20 years, only security assurances. This was true also for Ukraine after it joined NPT in December 1994.[6]

Ukraine could be a strong U.S. regional ally in central-eastern Europe. As a status quo power, it supports maintaining the territorial integrity of states and implementing a positive national minority policy with a Western-oriented culture. Ukraine provides a natural buffer against a newly resurgent Russia to prevent it from again becoming a threat to western and central Europe or a bridge between Europe and a democratic Russia. It is the key to the development of Russian democracy. If Russia were to absorb Ukraine, it could again become an empire and a dictatorship.[7]

At a conference on Ukraine and European Security in November 1993,[8] Ukrainian first deputy foreign minister Borys Tarasiuk outlined two sets of measures that the West should adopt toward Ukraine. On the economic side, the West should

- demonstrate a readiness to facilitate economic reforms, and then support them technically and financially
- provide public support within the IMF on the need for a stabilization fund for Ukraine's new currency, the *hryvnia*
- support Ukrainian associate membership of the EU when reforms are launched
- support the creation of a Fund for Nuclear Disarmament
- support the return of Ukraine's share of former Soviet assets unilaterally seized by Russia
- support political reform in Ukraine.

On security questions, first deputy foreign minister Tarasiuk added the following areas that should be raised. The West should

• block external support for the destabilization of, and territorial claims against, Ukraine
   • recognize external threats to Ukrainian independence
   • provide security guarantees from the five nuclear powers
   • provide public support for the creation of a Central European Zone of Stability and Cooperation as an interim mechanism
   • support Ukrainian security proposals for the Black Sea
region
   • support the equality of all successor states to the former
USSR
   • mediate Russian-Ukrainian disputes in the International
Court of Justice
   • reject the role of Russia as the peacekeeper on the territory
of the former USSR.

   U.S. and Western European support for these policy recommendations would go a long way toward improving relations
with Ukraine as well as enhancing regional stability and reform.

Russia and Central-Eastern Europe

Ukraine has to accept the uncomfortable fact that Russia will
always be more strategically important to the West for geopolitical, military, and economic reasons. Russia will have continued
interest in access to warm-water port facilities and even forward
basing rights. But the West has failed to fully address the interre-
latedness of security concerns in central-eastern Europe. Perceived Western indifference to the fate of Bosnia-Herzegovina
and the near total absence of criticism of Russian military involvement and integrationist policies toward the former USSR have
contributed to growing disillusionment with the West, while
sharpening Ukrainian security fears of being left to the mercy of
Russia. Ukraine, after all, correctly assumes that the West, which
has been reluctant even to send UN peacekeeping forces to the
former USSR, will not use military force to oppose Russian intervention in, say, the Crimea.
   But the West can, and should, support a dual-track policy

toward Russia and the former USSR. Current Western policy, which is to write off the Transcaucasus, Central Asia, and Moldova, while "drawing the line" at Ukraine and warning Russia away from the Baltic republics, has only encouraged Russia to become assertive in its integrationist policies while damaging its domestic reform program. It is doubtful that Russia, which has been allowed to conduct its "Monroe Doctrine" elsewhere, will halt at this mythical "line" drawn by the West in front of Ukraine.

An alternative Western policy that would require vision and an appreciation of the interlinking of security concerns in central-eastern Europe, should be to support the territorial integrity of the states of the former USSR and warn Russia that military interference will have dire diplomatic and economic consequences. This should be tempered by demands through the UN and OSCE that the non-Russian states of the former USSR implement favorable national minority policies. The West should encourage any Russian support for coethnics in Ukraine or elsewhere along Hungarian, and not Serbian, lines.

Although central European states, such as Poland and Hungary, regard Ukrainian independence as in their national interests, they have rejected proposals for a Zone of Security and Stability put forward by Kiev. The United States has quietly encouraged them to reject what they also perceive as an anti-Russian *cordon sanitaire*, which has also been quietly dropped by President Kuchma.

At the same time, there seems little recognition in central Europe's or the West's eyes that rejection of Ukrainian proposals for enhancing security in the region should be matched by other positive proposals. Central Europe's headlong rush to membership in Western institutions, such as NATO, will lead to Ukraine's being "left to its own devices and God's mercy," as Dmytro Pavlychko, then head of the parliamentary commission on foreign affairs, commented at a NATO seminar in Kiev in June 1993.

No solution to central Europe's security concerns will be comprehensive without dealing with Russian and Ukrainian security fears and threat perceptions. Yet, Western policymakers tend to neglect even taking into account Ukraine's views on central

Europe's membership in NATO, despite the fact that Ukraine borders four countries in central Europe (while Russia borders only one). Although the zone of security in Europe will move to Ukraine's western borders, if central Europe joins NATO, Ukraine will feel isolated and left to its own fate in the "Russian sphere of influence." This, in turn, will lead to either a national-ization of Ukrainian security policy (including nuclear weapons and again neglecting reform) or the reincorporation of Ukraine into a Russian-dominated CIS. In either case NATO and its new central European members will be faced by a hostile environment on its new eastern flank and a deterioration in their security.

Thus Ukrainian security is under dual pressure. On the one hand, NATO appears ready to expand in the short term into central Europe, bringing it right up to Ukraine's western borders with three countries. On the other, the abandoning of President Yeltsin by his former democratic allies in Russia during the Chechnya crisis in early 1995 has pointed to the acute instability of Ukraine's eastern neighbor, which seems prepared to reject reform and good relations with the West for traditional imperial-ism and Russian nationalism. In contrast, President Kuchma has taken Ukraine into 1995 with improved relations with the West, a radical program of reform, finalization of the nuclear question, and compromise to achieve domestic consensus.[9] These factors together should ensure that Ukraine remains central to European security and strategically vital to the United States.

A New Security Framework

The key to stabilizing, reforming, and denuclearizing Ukraine lies in improving Ukraine's security environment. The West will have to address the uncomfortable fact that a large proportion of the Russian leadership prefer Ukrainian dependence to independence or, at the very least, will question its sovereignty over the Crimea for a long time to come. If, as I have argued, a disintegrating Ukraine or one reincorporated within a new Russian empire is not in the West's interest, then the development of a new secu-rity relationship will have to be constructed between Ukraine and the West, principally with the United States.

The West will have to balance this policy of promoting Ukrainian security while not damaging relations with democratic Russia. A Russia that includes a reincorporated Ukraine would become an empire again, which traditionally has brought conflict with the West. In addition, to incorporate republics such as Ukraine into a Russian-dominated CIS would merely serve to water down the Russian reform process itself, distracting Russia from domestic affairs. This process is already under way, and it is not clear whether Russia will continue on its path of democratic reform.

Separating the former Soviet bloc into different zones would increase security for some countries while decreasing it for others. A new security architecture must be created for central-eastern Europe as a whole. Demands for Ukrainian denuclearization should not be regarded as a purely technical matter of proliferation, but should be part of the West's broadening dialogue and comprehensive political strategy toward the former USSR. Expanding NATO into central Europe must therefore take into account not only Russia's, but Ukraine's, security fears. The granting by the major international powers of permanent neutrality to Ukraine along the lines of Austria in 1955 should be considered as part of the process of NATO's expansion to Ukrainian borders.

A major component of this broadening dialogue has to include security questions. The interests of Ukraine and Russia can no longer be divorced—as they were for at least two years after the Soviet Union collapsed. Joint military training and exercises, regular consultations with both Russia and Ukraine on security matters, and the inclusion of both in a new regional security architecture is essential. The West should support Ukrainian ties to central Europe, not discourage them. An anti-Russian *cordon sanitaire* is an unlikely danger, but could be supported by the West in the event of resurgent Russian imperialism. Ukraine could back central European membership in NATO in return for central European support for its proposal to create a Zone of Security and Cooperation in central Europe as a temporary, overlapping mechanism.

A vital ingredient of this new security framework should be vigorous support for political and economic reform, particularly in those countries where it has only begun but is vital to alleviate domestic crisis. It is only by promoting political reform in Ukraine that a mandate for unpopular economic measures can be undertaken. Democratic groups should be strengthened to weaken the grip of national communists, who are ambivalent toward reform and have played their nationalist card to maintain their grip on power. Support for economic reform would create the conditions for the growth of a civil society and new middle class, which are the cornerstones of a Western society. Dealing with the economic crisis and hyperinflation may remove the breeding grounds for authoritarianism and separatism. This would be part of a process of promoting Westernization in Ukraine, which traditionally has no basis for a Slavophile anti-Western orientation.

Promoting the security of Russia and Ukraine within a new eastern European security architecture would tackle a dangerous conflict potentially awaiting Europe that would dwarf the conflict in the former Yugoslavia. To address this question now would guarantee a settlement, not a conflict, in the future. Ukraine and Russia will not resolve their deep and all-embracing disputes without Western assistance and arbitration, especially over the Black Sea Fleet and Crimea questions.

The West should continue to demand the withdrawal of Russian military bases from the former Soviet republics, not just the Baltic states but also others such as those in Ukraine and Moldova. The West should also oppose the use of Russian peacekeeping forces, which cannot be regarded as impartial and have often been instrumental in initially fanning the conflict.[10] Their conduct in Chechnya has proven how ill-equipped and brutal the Russian "peacekeeping forces" are. Perhaps Ukrainian peacekeeping forces could be used as an alternative under UN or OSCE aegis. After all, they have accumulated experience in Bosnia (5 Ukrainian soldiers have been killed there and 25 wounded) and would be regarded as more impartial.[11] Both Georgia and Moldova originally stated their preference for Ukrainian peacekeeping forces. In Azerbaijan an OSCE peacekeeping force could be made up of large numbers of Ukrainians as Baku is unlikely to accept Russians after their involvement in the Chechnya conflict.

NATO has been successful in both promoting stability and securing democracy in at least four member countries – Portugal, Spain, Greece, and Turkey. A new NATO designed to project Western values, promote stability, and cope with crisis management would be in a better position to help create the new security architecture for eastern Europe. In the medium to long term, NATO membership could be offered to Ukraine and Russia if Ukraine were to denuclearize and Russia to scale down its role as *gendarme* in the former USSR, while both continued the reform process.

At the same time that NATO considered including central European members, it would have to deal with eastern Europe in partnership. The North Atlantic Consultative Council (NACC) should be given peacekeeping and enforcement roles (possibly in cooperation with the OSCE), with particular emphasis on training for roles in central-eastern Europe, where many potential ethnic conflicts exist.[12]

NATO could strive to become the military arm of the OSCE, thereby giving it the legitimacy to play a pan-European role. Ukrainian peacekeeping forces would be more objective and possess no hidden geopolitical agenda, unlike Russian peacemaking forces. In the words of Zbigniew Brzezinski, "Russia as umpire is not very different from Russia as empire."[13]

Ukraine should be encouraged to support central Europe's membership in NATO in the short term on condition that its security requirements will also be taken into account. This should incorporate Western support for territorial integrity, internationally recognized national minority rights, and the reform process. It will also have to include greater Western sensitivity to Russian territorial claims and interference in the republics of the former USSR, a policy that is still lacking.[14]

It would not be in the West's interests to let Ukraine slide into isolationism. That would be a recipe for the nationalization of Ukraine's security policy and for instability in central and eastern Europe. Ukraine will push for full Western recognition and integration into European structures to obtain maximum leverage vis-à-vis Russia. Russian military bases, support for separatism, and coup d'etats in the new Arc of Crisis stretching along the northern rim of the Black Sea from Moldova to Azerbaijan place Ukraine under severe external pressure and enhance its security fears and threat perceptions. The West should thus promote a new security dialogue with Ukraine and construct a new security architecture in eastern, as well as central, Europe.

Postscript:
Ukraine Enters a New Era

Since the election of President Kuchma in July 1994, Ukraine has made tremendous progress in a number of key areas that threatened its survival as an independent state in 1993–1994. The legacy of former president Kravchuk's term in office (December 1991–July 1994) will be debated by future historians and political analysts. But his main credit is twofold. First, he was the main initiator in the dramatic events that led to the disintegration of the former USSR at the meeting of the three east Slavic leaders in Belarus on December 7–8, 1991. This followed his success in obtaining a high voter endorsement of more than 90 percent in the independence referendum a week earlier. Second, Kravchuk ensured a period of stability, continuity, and unity during Ukraine's crucial first year as an independent state by coopting the *ancien* regime in favor of independence. Ukraine, unlike other regions of the former USSR, thus did not witness domestic upheaval or ethnic conflict.

If Kravchuk, however, is historically remembered for divorcing Ukraine from the USSR, the economic stagnation and domestic crisis of 1993–1994 showed how he was unable to finish the task. Indeed, if he had been reelected in the summer of 1994, the domestic political and economic crisis may have undone his greatest achievement—independence. In contrast to his predecessor, Kuchma has shown that he possesses the political will, determination, and vision to transform Ukraine's Soviet political and economic system into a Western-style democracy and market economy. The launch of Kuchma's reform program in October 1994 is the first serious commitment to reform in the history of post-Soviet Ukraine, a factor recognized by Western governments and international financial institutions.

During Kuchma's first year in office, Ukraine successfully normalized relations with the West. As the U.S.–Ukrainian summit on May 11, 1995, showed, in contrast to the summit with President Yeltsin a day earlier in Moscow, no obstacles now exist to good relations between the West and Ukraine. Ukraine's agreement to close the Chornobyl nuclear plant, its launch of a reform program, its ratification of the NPT, its backing for the expansion of NATO in Central Europe up to its Western borders, and its support for not revising the CFE Treaty (Ukraine, like Russia, is discriminated against by the treaty's flank limits) have all been recognized as important factors by Western policymakers. They have also noted Ukraine's domestic peace and its importance as a status quo power to stability in central-eastern Europe and the Black Sea region. There are no domestic "Chechnyas," proposed deliveries of nuclear technology to rogue countries, or refusals to consider other nuclear treaties (such as START II) to cast doubt, at least in North America, on the strategic importance of Ukraine to the new geopolitical landscape of post-communist Europe.

The normalization of relations with Russia, another important plank of Kuchma's new program, has been less successful. The lingering dispute over the Black Sea Fleet cannot be resolved without U.S. mediation through the Trilateral Commission, established in January 1994 to coax Ukraine into ratifying START I. To remove the Crimea as a source of friction between Ukraine and Russia and as a potential source of regional instability requires U.S. mediation directed toward the eventual withdrawal of the Russian portion of the Black Sea Fleet from Ukraine and the demilitarization of the Crimean peninsula (except for domestic and border security forces). In addition, security assurances that support Ukraine's territorial integrity were provided by the nuclear powers–Russia included–in December 1994, leaving no obstacles to the international legal recognition of Ukraine's frontiers by Moscow in the proposed interstate treaty.

Four years into independence, Ukraine has begun a new lease on life under President Kuchma. Political and economic reform, together with the normalization of relations with the outside world, areas all linked closely, now deserve the West's full support. In contrast to the pessimism that in 1993–1994 surrounded Ukraine's ability to survive as an independent state, Ukraine has entered a new era in 1995 that will reflect its importance as a key linchpin of regional security and stability in Europe.

Notes

Notes to Chapter 1

1. For a comprehensive recent historical survey, one of the few that includes the modern period, see Orest Subtelny, *Ukraine: A History* (Toronto: University of Toronto Press, 1988).

2. See chapter 1, "Ukrainian Society on the Eve of the Revolution," in Bohdan Krawchenko, *Social Change and National Consciousness in Twentieth Century Ukraine* (London: Macmillan in association with St. Antony's College, Oxford, 1985), and John Basarab, *Pereiaslav 1654: A Historiographical Study* (Edmonton: Canadian Institute of Ukrainian Studies, 1982).

3. See Ivan L. Rudnytsky, "The Ukrainians in Galicia under Austrian Rule," *Austrian History Yearbook* 3, part 2 (1967): 394–429.

4. On Ukrainians in interwar Poland, see Jozef Lewandowski, "Kwestia ukrainska w 11 Rzeczpospolitej," *Aneks: kwartalnik polityczny*, no. 28 (1982): 97–122.

5. See John A. Armstrong, *Ukrainian Nationalism* (Littleton, Colorado: Ukrainian Academic Press, 1980).

6. See B. Krawchenko, "The Impact of Industrialisation on the Social Structure of Ukraine," *Canadian Slavonic Papers* 22, no. 3 (September 1980): 338–357.

7. See Robert Conquest, *The Harvest of Sorrow: Soviet Collectivisation and the Terror Famine* (London: Hutchinson, 1986).

8. Anatoliy Zlenko, "Independent Ukraine: Risk or Stability?" *RUSI Journal* (April 1992): 39.

9. Vasyl Hyrychenko, "National Interests: A Balance of Compromises and a Synthesis of Possibilities," *Viche* (Kiev), September 1992, p. 9. Another author, Volodymyr Lytvyn, argued that only Belarus did not harbor territorial claims against Ukraine (*Viche*, December 1992, p. 46, and *Viche*, March 1993, pp. 63–64).

10. See John Tedstrom, "The Economic Costs and Benefits of Independence for Ukraine," *Report on the USSR*, RL 500/90 (December 7, 1990).

11. See Mykola Ryabchuk, "Two Ukraines?" *East European Reporter* 5, no. 4 (July-August 1992): 18–22.

12. See two articles by Jaroslaw Martyniuk showing that the majority of the Ukrainian population are against border changes: "Ukrainian Independence and Territorial Integrity," and "Roundup: Attitudes toward Ukraine's Borders," *RFE/RL Research Report* 1, no. 13 (March 27, 1992) and no. 35 (September 4, 1992).

13. See Susan Stewart, "Ukraine's Policy toward Its Ethnic Minorities," *RFE/RL Research Report* 2, no. 36 (September 10, 1993).

14. *Demokratychna Ukraina* (Kiev), March 31, 1992.

15. *Demokratychna Ukraina*, April 9, 1992, and *Narodna Armiya* (Kiev), September 24, 1992.

16. *Respublika* (Kiev), March 13–19, 1993.

17. See Roman Solchanyk, "Russia, Ukraine, and the Imperial Legacy," *Post-Soviet Affairs* 9, no. 4 (October-December 1993): 337–374.

18. The comment is by B. Krawchenko, director of the Kiev-based Institute of Public Administration and Local Government (*Financial Times*, September 14, 1993). See also, Serhei Teleshun, "Will We Repeat 1918?" *Viche*, August 1993, pp. 42–45.

Notes to Chapter 2

1. See chapter 6, "The Inevitability of National Communism," in Alexander J. Motyl, *Sovietology, Rationality, Nationality: Coming to Grips with Nationalism in the USSR* (New York: Columbia University Press, 1990), 87–99.

2. See Yaroslav Bilinsky, "Mykola Skrypnyk and Petro Shelest: An Essay on the Persistence and Limits of National Communism," in Jeremy R. Azrael, ed., *Soviet Nationality Policies and Practices* (New York: Praeger Publishers, 1978), 105–143.

3. Kravchuk rose to high prominence in the CPU during the con-

servative Brezhnev era–that is, the "era of stagnation." He became second secretary of the CPU central committee in June 1990 but held this post only until he was elected chairman of the Ukrainian parliament four months later.

4. *Nezavisimaya Gazeta* (Moscow), January 12, 1991, and April 16, 1991.

5. The CPU was always hostile to Ukrainian independence. Those former members of the CPU who have remained hostile have joined groups subsequently established after the banning of the CPU in August 1991, such as the (Leninist) Socialist Party and (Stalinist) Communist Party. Although the majority of former CPU members did not rejoin any political party (only 150,000 out of 2.5 million members), in April 1993 the Labour Congress of Ukraine was established by some national communists as a "centrist" political force, reportedly with the support of former chairman of parliament Pliushch. *Holos Ukrainy* (Kiev), March 30, 1993.

6. Compiled by CSCE staff, *Implementation of the Helsinki Accords: Human Rights and Democratization in the Newly Independent States of the Former Soviet Union* (Washington, D.C.: Council for Security and Cooperation in Europe, 1993).

7. See Ben Shlomo, "The Return to History," *The Brookings Review*, Spring 1992, pp. 30–33.

8. *The Economist*, June 13, 1992. See also, Taras Kuzio, *Ukraine: The Unfinished Revolution*, European Security Study no. 16 (London: Institute for European Defence and Strategic Studies, 1992), 19–20.

9. Ihor Markov, "The Role of the President in the Ukrainian Political System," *RFE/RL Research Report* 2, no. 48 (December 3, 1993).

10. See A.N. Honcharenko and E.M. Lisitsyn, "Armed Forces of Ukraine and Problems of National Security," in Centre for Defence Studies, King's College, ed., *Brassey's Defence Yearbook 1993* (London: Brassey's, 1993), 155–156.

11. See Stephen Foye, "Civilian-Military Tension in Ukraine," *RFE/RL Research Report* 2, no. 25 (June 18, 1993).

12. "Concept of the Socio-Psychological Service of the Armed Forces of Ukraine," published in *Narodna Armiya*, January 22, 1993.

13. *Viche*, December 1992, p. 58.

14. See the interview with the head of the Department to Defend National Statehood and Society from Anti-Constitutional Acts as well as the Struggle against Terrorism, former Rukh leader, Viktor Burlakov, in *Uriadoviy Kurier* (Kiev), nos. 127–128 (August 21, 1993).

15. On the UUO see T. Kuzio, "Ukraine's Young Turks–The Union of Ukrainian Officers," *Jane's Intelligence Review*, January 1993.

16. See interview with Skipalsky in *Vechirniy Kiev*, July 23, 1993.

17. *The Ukrainian Weekly*, October 10, 1993, and *UNIAN news agency* (Kiev), December 14, 1993.

18. *The Ukrainian Weekly*, October 17, 1993.

19. See Roman Solchanyk, "The Politics of State Building: Centre-Periphery Relations in Post-Soviet Ukraine," *Europe-Asia Studies* 46, no. 1 (January-February 1994): 47–68.

20. See Ustina Markus, "Belarus Debates Security Pacts as a Cure for Military Woes," *RFE/RL Research Report* 2, no. 25 (June 18, 1993).

21. See Roman Solchanyk, "Ukraine's Search for Security," *RFE/RL Research Report* 2, no. 21 (May 21, 1993); Taras Kuzio, "Ukraine and Its Future Security," *Jane's Intelligence Review*, December 1993; and Frank Umbach, "The Security of an Independent Ukraine," *Jane's Intelligence Review*, March 1994.

22. See Taras Kuzio, "Ukrainian Paramilitaries" and "Paramilitaries in Ukraine," *Jane's Intelligence Review*, December 1992 and March 1994.

23. On the extra questions proposed by the Donbas for the September 1993 referendum, see *Holos Ukrainy*, August 3, 12, and 13, 1993. See also Andrew Wilson, "The Growing Challenge to Kiev from the Donbas," *RFE/RL Research report* 2, no. 33 (August 20, 1993).

24. *UNIAN news agency*, August 30, 1993.

25. *Radio Ukraine*, March 16, 1994.

26. On the pre-election situations in Donets'k and Luhans'k, see *Post Postup* (L'viv), no. 43 (November 25-December 1, 1994), and *Narodna Hazeta* (Kiev), no. 8 (February 1994). See also, Monika Jung, "The Donbas Factor in the Ukrainian Elections," *RFE/RL Research Report* 3, no. 12 (March 25, 1994).

27. The referendum results are given by *UNIAN news agency*, March 31, 1994. On Donbas regionalism, see *UPI*, February 22, 1994.

28. See R. Solchanyk, "Crimea's Presidential Elections," *RFE/RL Research Report* 3, no. 11 (March 18, 1994).

29. *Reuters*, February 19, 1994.

30. See Elizabeth Teague, "Russia and Tatarstan Sign Power-Sharing Treaty," *RFE/RL Research Report* 3, no. 14 (April 8, 1994).

31. *Holos Ukrainy*, March 1, 1992.

32. *Reuters*, March 15 and 16, 1994.

33. See Leonid Tsilyunsky, "Crimea-94: Abkhaz Variant?" *Post Postup*, April 8-14, 1994.

34. *Reuters*, April 10, 1994.

35. *Ukrainian Radio*, March 29, 1994, and *The Ukrainian Weekly*, April 3, 1994.

36. *Uriadoviy Kurier*, no. 28 (February 23, 1993).

37. Ukraine received a total of 83 points, followed by the Baltic Republics (79) and Russian Federation (72). See Dr. Otto Storf, ed., *The Soviet Union at the Crossroads: Facts and Figures on the Soviet Republics* (Frankfurt: Deutsche Bank AG, npd).

38. David Marples, "Ukraine's Economic Prospects," *Report on the USSR* 3, no. 40 (October 4, 1991).

39. *Post Postup*, no. 44 (November 24–30, 1992).

40. See Mykhail Beletskiy, "The June Strikes: Origins and Analysis," *Ukrainskiy Ohliadach* (Kiev), no. 8 (1993).

41. *Uriadoviy Kurier*, February 1, 1994.

42. *UNIAN news agency*, November 10, 1993.

43. *AP*, March 1, 1994. See also, Robert Seely, "Ukraine Backtracks on Reform, Boosts Subsidies to State-Run Farms," *The Washington Post*, February 23, 1994.

44. *Narodna Armiya*, October 22, 1992.

45. *Demokratychna Ukraina*, March 17, 1994.

46. *Uriadoviy Kurier*, nos. 36–37 (March 11, 1993). In another poll conducted in Kiev oblast, 52 percent believed the mafia were running Ukraine, 36.3 percent thought the former nomenklatura, 23.4 percent directors and chairmen of collective farms. Only 18, 8.2, and 5.9 percent respectively believed that the president, government, and parliament were running Ukraine (*Holos Ukrainy*, August 13, 1993).

47. *Pravda Ukrainy* (Kiev), April 15, 1993. See also, *Journal of Commerce*, no. 1 (March 1993).

48. On Iranian-Ukrainian relations, see *Vechirniy Kiev*, February 11, 1994.

49. *Silski Visti* (Kiev), February 2, 1993.

50. Details of the agreements made with Oman can be found in *Uriadoviy Kurier*, no. 55 (April 13, 1993).

51. *Holos Ukrainy*, March 31, 1993.

52. *The Guardian*, September 28, 1993. See interview with former Premier Yefim Zvyahilsky in *Uriadoviy Kurier*, no. 135 (September 7, 1993).

Notes to Chapter 3

1. See *Kommunist Ukrainy* (Kiev), no. 11 (1990): 62–69.

2. *The Economist*, June 15, 1991.

3. *Kievskyi Visnyk* (Kiev), September 13, 1991. See also, Natalie Melnyczuk, "Ukraine Develops an Independent Foreign Policy: The First Year," *Report on the USSR* 3, no. 43 (October 25, 1991).

4. *Silski Visti* (Kiev), May 8, 1992.

5. *Nezavisimaya Gazeta,* December 23, 1992. See also, the criticism of a lack of a Ukrainian foreign policy serving Ukraine's national interests by former Gorbachev adviser on nationality affairs and leading Ukrainian communist Borys Oliynyk (*Holos Ukrainy,* February 5, 1993).

6. *Nezavisimaya Gazeta,* December 23, 1992.

7. *Holos Ukrainy,* March 20, 1993, and July 10, 1993, and *Intel News* (Kiev), July 5, 1993. A military doctrine was adopted in October 1993 (see chapter 4), but no national security program has yet been formulated. Zlenko outlined Ukrainian security policy to parliament in the same month (*Holos Ukrainy,* July 20, 1993). See also, Leonid Kravchuk, "A New Ukraine in a New Europe," *Polityka i Chas* (Kiev), no. 2 (1993).

8. *Viche,* March 1993.

9. *Polityka i Chas,* no. 2 (1993).

10. *Holos Ukrainy,* August 26, 1992, and *The Ukrainian Weekly,* October 11, 1992.

11. *Wall Street Journal,* January 7-8, 1994.

12. *The Ukrainian Weekly,* February 13, 1994. See also favorable comments in *Narodna Armiya,* February 11, 1992, and *Holos Ukrainy,* February 19, 1992.

13. *Ukrainian Radio* (Kiev), March 25, 1994.

14. *AP,* February 7, 1994, and *Reuters,* February 8, 1994.

15. See Peter van Ham, *Ukraine, Russia and European Security: Implications for Western Policy,* Chaillot Papers 13 (Paris: Institute for Security Studies, Western European Union, February 1994).

16. On the growth of anti-Americanism in Ukraine, see Mary Mycio, "America Losing Luster in Ukraine," *Los Angeles Times,* June 1, 1993, and Anne Applebaum, "The Comfort of Missiles," *The Spectator,* June 26, 1993.

17. *Financial Times,* May 7, 1993.

18. *New York Times,* June 4, 1993.

19. See Alexei K. Pushkov, "Letter from Eurasia: Russia and America: The Honeymoon's Over," *Foreign Policy,* no. 93 (Winter 1993-1994): 76-90.

20. A. Kozyrev, "Russia and the United States: Partnership Not Premature, but Overdue," *Izvestiya,* March 11, 1994. See also, Michael R.

Gordon, "Perry Says Caution Is Vital to Russian Partnership," *New York Times,* March 15, 1994, and Steven Greenhouse, "U.S. to Russia: A Tougher Tone and a Shifting Glance," *New York Times,* March 21, 1994.

21. Steven Greenhouse, "U.S. Issues a Warning to Russia to Keep Economic Reform Going," *New York Times,* January 25, 1994.

22. Editorial, "The Spy Case: The Fallout," and Charles Krauthammer, "Spying Non-Scandal: A Minor Event Signalling the End of the Honeymoon," *Washington Post,* February 25, 1994.

23. Daniel Wiliams, "U.S. Shifts Policy Focus to Russian Border States: Moscow Troops, Ukraine Are Emphasized," *Washington Post,* February 5, 1994; Mark M. Nelson, "Russia's Rising Assertiveness Stirs Concern," *Wall Street Journal,* March 4, 1994; and James Adams, "U.S. Cools Support for 'Spent Yeltsin,'" *Sunday Times,* March 20, 1994.

24. Dmitri Simes, "Is Yeltsin Losing His Grip?" *New York Times,* March 6, 1994, and Philip Zelikow, "Beyond Boris Yeltsin," *Foreign Affairs* 73, no. 1 (January-February 1994): 44–55.

25. Zbigniew Brzezinski, "The Premature Partnership," *Foreign Affairs* 73, no. 2 (March-April 1994): 67–82, and "A Tale of Two Bears," *The Economist,* March 12, 1994.

26. *New York Times,* March 25, 1994, and *Washington Post,* April 14, 1994. See also, Lally Weymouth, "U.S. Can Calm Ukrainian Jitters," *Washington Post,* January 24, 1994, and Robert Seely, "A Bigger Role for 'Little Russia,'" *The Independent,* March 8, 1994.

27. Daniel Williams, "Christopher Discerns 'Good Signs' in Speech Despite Its Tough Tone," *Washington Post,* February 25, 1994.

28. See Oleksandr Dubyna, "USA-Ukraine: From Pressure to a 'New Partnership'?" *Polityka i Chas,* no. 12 (1993), and Steven Greenhouse, "Clinton Vows to Improve Relations with Ukraine," *New York Times,* March 5, 1994.

29. *Reuters,* March 5, 1994, and *Financial Times,* March 7, 1994.

30. Conversation with Roland Freudenstein, Forschungsinstitut der Deutschen Gesellschaft fur Auswartige Politik (DGAP), Bonn, January 1993. This, of course, excluded the specialist staff of the U.S.-funded RFE/RL Research Institute then based in Munich.

31. *Demokratychna Ukraina,* May 16, 1992.

32. *Reuters,* February 5, 1994.

33. *Kievskoye Vedomosti* (Kiev), February 24, 1994. Oleksandr Motsyk, Ukraine's UN representative, spoke in favor of expanding the UN Security Council to 20 to 25 members on March 18, 1994.

34. *DPA news agency,* April 11, 1994.

35. *Financial Times,* October 23, 1991.

36. The statement and draft treaty are published in *Uriadoviy Kurier,* no. 104 (July 17, 1993).

37. *Holos Ukrainy,* June 24, 1993, and September 23, 1993.

38. See Stephen M. Meyer, "The Military," in Timothy J. Colton and Robert Legvold, eds., *After the Soviet Union: From Empire to Nations* (New York: W.W. Norton and Co., 1992), 113-146. The Russian leadership, after all, was initally reluctant to militarily quell the separatist Chechens or Tatars, let alone think of militarily attacking Ukraine.

39. These figures were given by the deputy chief of the CIS General Staff, Col.-Gen. L.V. Kuznetsov (*Nezavisimaya Gazeta,* May 7, 1992).

40. See John Morrison, "Pereyaslav and After: The Russian-Ukrainian Relationship," *International Affairs* 69, no. 4 (October 1993): 677-704; and William H. Kincade and Natalie Melnyczuk, "Eurasian Letter: Unneighbourly Neighbours," *Foreign Policy,* no. 94 (Spring 1994): 84-104.

41. *Izvestiya,* January 16, 1993.

42. *Respublika,* April 3-9, 1993.

43. *Le Monde,* June 7-8, 1992. Hence Ukraine has insisted that all its treaties with neighbors include a clause renouncing all territorial changes, forceful and peaceful.

44. See Suzanne Crow, "Russia Seeks Leadership in Regional Peacekeeping," *RFE/RL Research Report* 2, no. 15 (April 9, 1993).

45. *Izvestiya,* August 7, 1992. See also, Wendy Slater, "The Center Right in Russia," *RFE/RL Research Report,* no. 34 (August 27, 1993).

46. *Financial Times,* December 14, 1993. See also, Radek Sikorski, "Mr Hurd's Short Memory," *Spectator,* January 15, 1994.

47. *Izvestiya,* October 8, 1993.

48. See the criticism of the Russian military doctrine by Ihor Kharchenko, head of the Political Analysis and Planning department of the Ukrainian Foreign Ministry. *Polityka i Chas,* no. 1 (1994).

49. See Fiona Hill and Pamela Jewett, *Back in the USSR: Russia's Intervention in the Internal Affairs of the Former Soviet Republics and Their Implications for United States Policy towards Russia,* Strengthening Democratic Institutions Project (Cambridge, Mass.: John F. Kennedy School of Government, Harvard University, January 1994).

50. *Pravda,* January 30, 1992.

51. Chairman of the Russian Officers Union Stanislav Terekhov claimed that his organization's 10,000 members supported the National Salvation Front (*Sunday Times,* October 25, 1992).

52. *Wall Street Journal*, April 5, 1994.

53. *Izvestiya*, May 26, 1992.

54. See Konstantin Pleshakov, "The Crimea: Where Are Stupid Nationalists Pushing Us?" *New Times International* (Moscow), no. 34 (1993); and Taras Kuzio, *Russia-Crimea-Ukraine: Triangle of Conflict*, Conflict Study 267 (London: Research Institute for the Study of Conflict and Terrorism, 1994).

55. *Respublika*, no. 23 (November 4–10, 1993).

56. *Komsomolskaya Pravda* (Moscow), January 22, 1992.

57. *Washington Times*, April 7, 1994.

58. The Ukrainian responses appeared in *Holos Ukrainy*, July 13, 1993. See also, *Financial Times* and *Guardian*, July 10, 1993; and the long article by Bohdan Horyn entitled "Sevastopol: An Undeclared War," in the newspaper of the Ministry of Defence, *Narodna Armiya*, March 27, 1993.

59. See the statement by the Labour Party that appealed to the Russian parliament to draw back from its decree. *Robitnycha Hazeta* (Kiev), July 21, 1993.

60. *Moscow News*, no. 47 (1992), and *Nezavisimaya Gazeta*, March 5, 1993. With a population five times larger than Belarus, Ukraine received 20 million tonnes of oil in 1993, only 4 million more than Belarus obtained (*Economist*, February 20, 1993). The use of energy supplies to apply pressure upon other former Soviet republics has been publicly admitted by President Yeltsin on many occasions. See *Christian Science Monitor*, June 21, 1993, and *Independent*, July 10, 1993.

61. *Financial Times*, February 19, 1993.

62. Sixty-three percent of Kievites and fifty-eight percent of L'vivites believed that military conflict was likely in the near future with Russia. *Post Postup*, no. 2 (February 10–16, 1994).

63. See Editorial, "The Plot to Recapture Ukraine," *New York Times*, March 14, 1994. Karaganov told a Moscow conference that "Russia faces a choice: that between the recreation of a Union and the imposition of an empire." Alexander Tsipko, a leading Russian philosopher, argued that Russians could not live only within the borders of the Russian Federation. The only "Russia" possible would be that associated with the territory of the former USSR (*Financial Times*, April 18, 1994).

64. *Washington Post*, March 1, 1994.

65. *Washington Times*, March 11, 1994.

66. See Alfred A. Reisch, "Hungarian-Ukrainian Relations Continue to Develop," *RFE/RL Research Report* 2, no. 16 (April 16, 1993).

67. *Polska w Europie* (Warsaw), no. 9 (July-September 1992). See also, Jan B. de Weydenthal, "Poland's Eastern Policy," *RFE/RL Research Report* 3, no. 7 (February 18, 1994).

68. *Post Postup,* no. 10 (April 8-14, 1994).

69. *UNIAR News Agency* (Kiev), February 25, 1994.

70. See "Romanian-Ukrainian Misunderstanding—*cui prodest?*" *News from Ukraine,* no. 5 (1994).

71. See Vladimir Socor, "Another Major Setback for Pro-Romanian Forces," *RFE/RL Research Report* 2, no. 9 (February 26, 1993).

72. It is not clear if the rhetoric of Romania's leaders is backed up by a genuine commitment to reunification as Moldovan demands for autonomous status (as the condition for acceptance of reunification) within Romania would fuel Hungarian demands for similar treatment in Transylvania, thereby ending Bucharest's traditional policy of maintaining a unitary state.

73. Helsinki Watch has reported that all parties to the Moldovan conflict have "committed acts of violence in defiance of international humanitarian law." See *Human Rights in Moldova: The Turbulent Dniester* (Washington, New York: Helsinki Watch, March 1993).

74. *Respublika,* July 3, 1993.

75. Vladimir Socor, "The Fourteenth Army in Moldova: There to Stay?" *RFE/RL Research Report* 2, no. 25 (June 18, 1993).

76. *Ostankino Television* (Moscow) interview with Lebed, September 5, 1993. See also, *Ekho Moskvy* (Moscow), September 2, 1993, and *Basapress* (Chisinau), September 7, 1993.

77. *Rossiiskie Vesti* (Moscow), February 2, 1994.

78. *Nezavisimaya Gazeta,* January 18, 1994.

79. See "Brotherly Mutual Understanding," *Uriadoviy Kurier,* nos. 42-43 (March 17, 1994).

80. See "Our Special Partner. Ukraine-Moldova: Neighbourly Relations on an Inter-State Legal Basis," *Polityka i Chas,* no. 1 (1994).

81. Meanwhile, Romania accused the Moldovan leadership of treachery and of "serving Moscow's interests" (*Reuters,* April 12 and 14, 1994).

82. *Sfatul Tarii* (Chishinau), January 20, 1994. In a manner similar to Latvia and Estonia, Moldova demanded that Russian troops complete their withdrawal by July 1994. Instead, an agreement was reached to pull out Russian forces over three years, but it is unclear if Russia will stick to this timetable as it has already been rejected by the State Duma in a unanimous vote.

83. Ustina Markus, "Conservatives Remove Belarusian Leader," *RFE/RL Research Report* 3, no. 8 (February 25, 1994). See also, David R. Marples, "Belarus: The Illusion of Stability," *Post-Soviet Affairs* 9, no. 3 (July-September 1993): 253–277.

84. *ITAR-TASS*, March 11, 1994. On Belarusian denuclearization, which will be the first of the four former Soviet republics to be completely free of strategic nuclear weapons. See *Izvestiya*, March 17, 1994.

85. *ITAR-TASS*, March 16, 1994.

86. *Lithuanian Radio* (Vilnius), February 8, 1994. The comments were made by Kravchuk on a visit to Lithuania in February 1994.

87. *Holos Ukrainy*, May 6, 1992.

88. *Narodna Armiya*, July 17, 1993.

89. *Holos Ukrainy*, March 23, 1993. The declaration on the creation of the BSECA is reprinted in *Polityka i Chas*, no. 1 (1993).

90. The second session of the BSECA was held in May 1993 and the second session of the Parliamentary Assembly of the BSECA in November 1993 without the participation of Russia. See *ITAR-TASS*, November 29, 1993, and *Uriadoviy Kurier*, no. 174 (December 4, 1993).

91. Daniel A. Connelly, "Black Sea Economic Cooperation," *RFE/RL Research Report* 3, no. 26 (July 1, 1994): 35.

92. *Tehran Times*, May 13, 1993. The Memorandum on Understanding and Cooperation between the Iranian and Ukrainian parliaments is printed in *Holos Ukrainy*, May 19, 1993.

93. *Vechirnyi Kiev*, December 29, 1993. See also, Taras Kuzio, "Ukraine's Arms Exports," *Jane's Intelligence Review*, February 1994.

94. Nazarbayev has publicly stated that "any talk about protecting Russians living in Kazakhstan reminds one of the times of Hitler, who also started off with the question of the protection of Sudenten Germans." *Interfax*, November 24, 1993.

95. Nazarbayev announced this on his visit to Kiev, which took place on the eve of his U.S. visit. He wanted U.S. mediation because he was inclined "not to trust very much" the Russians (*Izvestiya*, January 22, 1994).

96. The declaration is printed in *Uriadoviy Kurier*, no. 14 (January 25, 1994).

97. *Washington Post*, February 8, 1994.

98. *Pravda Ukrainy*, March 31, 1992.

99. *PTI News Agency* (New Delhi), April 15, 1994.

100. *Robitnycha Hazeta*, October 28, 1992.

101. *Polityka i Chas,* no. 1 (1993).

102. Ustina Markus, "Ukrainian-Chinese Relations: Slow but Steady Progress," *RFE/RL Research Report* 2, no. 45 (November 12, 1993).

103. See "Russian Hardliners Demand Soviet Union Back," *Reuters,* March 17, 1994.

104. *ITAR-TASS,* March 29, 1994, and *Krasnaya Zvezda* (Moscow), April 5, 1994.

105. *Reuters,* April 14, 1994.

106. *Interfax* (Moscow, February 28, 1994) first reported the announcement by Russian General Staff Chief Mikhail Kolesnikov. The Yeltsin decree was issued on April 7 (*ITAR-TASS,* April 7, 1994, and *Izvestiya,* April 8, 1994).

107. See "Russia's Sphere of Influence," *Foreign Report (The Economist),* September 16, 1993, and "Great Russia Revives," *The Economist,* September 18, 1993.

108. Stankevich was reported as telling foreign diplomats not to bother opening embassies in Kiev because they would soon become only consulates again anyway (*The Economist,* March 13, 1993, and *Financial Times,* March 17, 1993).

Notes to Chapter 4

1. See Bohdan Pyskir, "The Silent Coup: The Building of Ukraine's Military," *European Security* 2, no. 1 (spring 1993): 140-161, and Taras Kuzio, "Nuclear Weapons and Military Policy in Independent Ukraine," *Harriman Institute Forum* 6, no. 9 (May 1993).

2. See Roy Allison, *Military Forces in the Soviet Successor States,* Adelphi Paper 280 (London: Brassey's for the IISS, 1993).

3. Taras Kuzio, "Ukraine's Military Industrial Plan," *Jane's Intelligence Review,* August 1994.

4. See *The Military Balance, 1991-1992* (London: Brassey's for the IISS, 1992), 86-87. Corrupt Ukrainian military officials allegedly supplied large numbers of aircraft and helicopters to Croatia in 1992-1994.

5. *Krasnaya Zvezda,* November 4, 1992.

6. *Narodna Armiya,* November 3, 1992.

7. Ibid., February 6, 1993.

8. Ibid., March 24, 1993.

9. Ibid., February 16, 1994.

10. Ukraine inherited six shipyards that once supported the Soviet

navy. In November 1992 Russia forwarded a proposal, "Cooperation on the Construction and Repair of Vessels and Naval Equipment for the Russian Navy."

11. See interview with Kozhyn in *Holos Ukrainy*, December 19, 1992, and Col. Mykhail Slobodianiuk, "What Kind of Fleet Do We Need?" *Narodna Armiya*, January 6–7, 1993. The uniforms and insignia of the Ukrainian Navy were printed in *Narodna Armiya*, December 30, 1992.

12. See interview with Pylypenko in *Post Postup*, no. 44 (November 24–30, 1992).

13. *Krasnaya Zvezda*, March 4, 1994.

14. See Steven Zaloga, "Strategic Forces of the SNG," *Jane's Intelligence Review*, February 1992.

15. See the Russian military condemnation of this move in *Rossiyskaya Gazeta* (Moscow), July 22, 1993.

16. *Financial Times*, March 15, 1992. Other reports, however, indicated that tactical nuclear missiles remained on the Black Sea Fleet as late as December 1992 (*Silski Visti*, January 6, 1993). This information corroborates that received by the author on a visit to the Crimea in August 1992.

17. See Charles Dick, "The Military Doctrine of Ukraine," *Jane's Intelligence Review*, March 1994.

18. *Holos Ukrainy*, October 29, 1993.

19. See the resolution of the State Committee to deal with Defence of the State Borders of Ukraine in *Holos Ukrainy*, December 5, 1992.

20. See Taras Kuzio, "The Ukrainian National Guard," *Jane's Intelligence Review*, May 1993.

21. See *Narodna Armiya*, February 27, March 5, 1993, and *Holos Ukrainy*, February 12, 1993, and March 19, 1993.

22. *Holos Ukrainy*, January 10, 1992.

23. *Narodna Armiya*, September 29, 1992.

24. Ibid., March 11, 1993.

25. *Narodna Armya*, April 2, 1993. See also the Statute of the Ukrainian National Fund for Social Guarantees of Servicemen and Veterans of the Armed Forces in *Narodna Armiya*, January 23, 1993.

26. *Narodna Hazeta*, September 7, 1993.

27. *Demokratychna Ukraina*, August 10, 1993.

28. The only study conducted of this is R.A. Woff, *Ukrainian Military Educational System. 1992–1993. K13* (Camberley: RMA Sand-

hurst, Soviet Studies Research Centre, 1992). A list of the newly re-formed military academies is published in *Narodna Armiya*, October 15, 1992.

29. *Holos Ukrainy*, April 8, 1993.

30. *Narodna Armiya*, July 1, 1992.

31. A history of the Black Sea Fleet can be found in Douglas L. Clarke, "The Saga of the Black Sea Fleet," *RFE/RL Research Report* 1, no. 4 (January 24, 1992).

32. *The Guardian*, January 10, 1992.

33. *Postfactum* (Moscow), March 24, 1992.

34. See Sir James Eberle, "Russia and Ukraine—What to Do with the Black Sea Fleet?" *The World Today* 48, nos. 8-9 (August-September 1992).

35. The Russian lawyer Genaddiy Melkov argued as early as February 1992 that Sevastopol should be given a special status "like West Berlin" and Russia, "should retain its rights for Sevastopol, irrespective of whether Ukraine remains in the commonwealth or leaves it." *Rossiyskaya Gazeta* (Moscow), February 14, 1992. Other reports have testified to the fact that it is not the status of the fleet that is most pressing, but whether Sevastopol will be home to the Russian and Ukrainian Fleets after 1995 (*Nezavisimaya Gazeta*, April 16, 1993).

36. Russia continued to insist at these meetings on only giving Ukraine 20 percent of the Fleet (*Holos Ukrainy*, April 30, 1992).

37. The Agreement is translated by the *Russian Information Agency—Novosti* (London) no. 160 (August 3, 1992).

38. The cadets who had taken the Russian oath were later transferred to St. Petersburg and Kalingrad (*Narodna Armiya*, April 15, 1993).

39. See ITAR-TASS, January 21-22, 1993, and *Holos Ukrainy*, April 6, 1993.

40. *Daily Telegraph*, May 25, 1993.

41. Kozyrev's statement from *Interfax* (Moscow), December 7, 1993; Luzhkov's statement from *The Ukrainian Weekly*, January 11, 1995.

42. *UNIAN news agency* (Kiev), September 9, 1993. On the Massandra summit, see Bohdan Nahaylo, "The Massandra Summit and Ukraine," *RFE/RL Research Report* 2, no. 37 (September 17, 1993).

43. *Narodna Armiya*, July 14, 1993, and *Uriadoviy Kurier*, July 17, 1993.

44. *Washington Post*, April 12, 1994.

45. *Reuters*, April 15, 1994.

46. The Lisbon Protocols and Letter from Kravchuk to Bush are reprinted in *Arms Control Today*, June 1992, pp. 34–36.

47. *Moscow News*, no. 42 (1992) and *Nezavisimaya Gazeta*, October 24, 1992.

48. *Den* (Moscow), no. 5 (February 7–13, 1993).

49. See Philip Zelikow, "Ownership and Control over CIS Nuclear Forces," in Graham Allison, Ashton B. Carter, Steven Miller, and Philip Zelikow, *Cooperative Denuclearization: From Pledges to Deeds,* CSIA Studies in International Security no. 2 (Cambridge, MA: Center for Science and International Affairs, John F. Kennedy School of Government, Harvard University, 1993), 72–78.

50. See *Press Release no. 48/1992* (November 10, 1992) of the Embassy of Ukraine, Washington, D.C.

51. *Nezavisimaya Gazeta*, January 11, 1993, and *Reuters*, May 14, 1993.

52. See interview with Pavlychko in *Holos Ukrainy*, July 30, 1993.

53. Kravchuk and Pavlychko argued that START I and the Lisbon Protocols did not obligate Ukraine to destroy the SS-24 missiles (*Holos Ukrainy*, July 30, 1993). Although they supported parliamentary ratification of START I, consideration of accession to the NPT regime would not take place until 1995. See also, *Izvestiya*, August 12, 1993, and *International Herald and Tribune*, July 31-August 1, 1993.

54. See John J. Mearsheimer, "The Case for a Ukrainian Nuclear Deterrent," and Steven E. Miller, "The Case against a Ukrainian Nuclear Deterrent," *Foreign Affairs* 72, no. 3 (summer 1993): 50–80, and "Kiev and the Bomb: Ukrainians Reply," *Foreign Affairs* 72, no. 4 (autumn 1993): 183–187.

55. *Washington Post*, July 28, 1993.

56. *Izvestiya*, July 16, 1993.

57. *Financial Times*, May 7, 1993.

58. *Holos Ukrainy*, February 17, 1992. Although Tarasiuk argued against holding on to nuclear weapons, he still demanded security guarantees and "justifiable compensation" for disarmament. See his interview in *Nezavisimaya Gazeta*, January 11, 1993. But Konstantin Krischenko, head of the Foreign Ministry Department on Arms Control and Disarmament, believed that ratification of START I did not even reflect Ukrainian interests (*Christian Science Monitor*, January 4, 1993).

59. *Uriadoviy Kurier*, no. 19 (February 6, 1993).

60. *Nezavisimaya Gazeta*, May 29, 1993.

61. John W.R. Lepingwell, "How Much Is a Warhead Worth?" *RFE/RL Research Report* 2, no. 8 (February 19, 1993): 53.

62. For various estimates ranging between $2–3 billion, see *Holos Ukrainy*, February 3, 1993; *ITAR-TASS*, April 23, 1993; and *The Ukrainian Weekly*, April 18, 1993.

63. See Martin J. DeWing, *The Ukrainian Nuclear Arsenal: Problems of Command, Control, and Maintenance*, Working Paper No. 3, Program for Nonproliferation Studies (Monterey: Institute of International Studies, October 1993).

64. *Holos Ukrainy*, April 17, 1992.

65. *Holos Ukrainy*, December 16, 1992, and *Narodna Armiya*, December 17, 1992.

66. *Time*, April 19, 1993.

67. See Steven Zaloga, "The CIS Nuclear Weapons Industry," *Jane's Intelligence Review*, September 1992.

68. Kurt M. Campbell, Ashton B. Carter, Steven E. Miller, and Charles A. Zraket, *Soviet Nuclear Fission: Control of the Nuclear Arsenal in a Disintegrating Soviet Union*, CSIA Studies in International Security 1 (Cambridge, Mass.: Center for Science and International Affairs, John F. Kennedy School of Government, Harvard University, 1991), p. 34 and p. 108.

69. *Izvestiya* and *Reuters*, February 22, 1994.

70. *Holos Ukrainy*, January 19, 1994.

71. *UPI*, January 26, 1994.

72. *Holos Ukrainy*, February 5, 1994. See also, J.W.R. Lepingwell, "Ukrainian Parliament Removes START-1 Conditions," *RFE/RL Research Report* 3, no. 8 (February 25, 1994).

73. The first 25-tonne consignment of enriched uranium was delivered to Europe's largest nuclear power station at Zaporizhzhia in mid-April. Russia was committed to deliver 100 tonnes within ten months (*Reuters*, April 14, 1994).

74. The law on Ukraine's ratification of the NPT is published in *Uriadoviy Kurier*, nos. 179–180 (November 22, 1994).

75. A copy of the declaration is in the possession of the author. See also *Radio Ukraine*, December 6, 1994.

Notes to Chapter 5

1. See Alexander J. Motyl, *Dilemmas of Independence: Ukraine after Totalitarianism* (New York: Council on Foreign Relations, 1993).

2. The national communist "Party of Power" has roughly divided between those who adopt a nationalist line, grouped around former

speaker of the Ukrainian parliament Pliushch, who launched the Labour Congress of Ukraine, and former president Kravchuk. The pro-
Russian/CIS orientation, which won the presidential elections in July
1994 with a small majority, is divided into pro- and anti-reform groups.
The pro-reform group within the pro-Russian/CIS orientation is led
by current president Kuchma, together with New Ukraine and the
Inter-Regional Bloc of Reforms. The pro-Russian/CIS anti-reform lobby
is represented by the communist/socialist/agrarian factions in the new
parliament.

3. See the article by Andrei Kozyrev, Russian foreign minister,
in *Nezavisimaya Gazeta*, September 22, 1993. See also, Roy Allison,
Peacekeeping in the Soviet Successor States, Chaillot Papers 18 (Paris: Institute for Security Studies, Western European Union, November 1994).

4. See a lengthy article by Serfity Pinchrov, director of the National Institute of Strategic Studies, on Ukrainian-Russian relations in
Holos Ukrainy (November 16 and 18, 1994).

5. See his interview given to *Interfax News Agency* as quoted in the
Boston Globe, September 15, 1993.

6. *Kievskoye Vedomosti*, March 24, 1994.

7. See Eugene B. Rumer, "Eurasia Letter: Will Ukraine Return to
Russia?" *Foreign Policy*, no. 96 (Fall 1994): 129–144.

8. The conference was organized by the Stiftung Wissenschaft und
Politik (SWP) and Rand Corporation in Ebenhausen between November 21–23, 1993, entitled "The Ukraine in Future European Architecture and Security Environment."

9. See Taras Kuzio, "Ukraine since the Elections–From Romanti-
cism to Pragmatism," *Jane's Intelligence Review*, December 1994.

10. See Fiona Hill and Pamela Jewett, *Back in the USSR: Russia's
Intervention in the Internal Affairs of the Former Soviet Republics and the
Implications for United States Policy toward Russia* (Cambridge, MA: John
F. Kennedy School of Government, Harvard University, 1994).

11. The Serbs had asked for Ukrainian UN peacekeeping troops
for Goradze because of their realization that Russian peacekeeping
forces "make the Muslims nervous" (*Reuters*, April 13, 1994).

12. See Ronald D. Asmus, Richard L. Kugler, and F. Stephen
Larrabee, "Building a New NATO," *Foreign Affairs* 72, no. 4 (autumn
1993): 28–40.

13. Zbigniew Brzezinski, "The Premature Partnership," *Foreign
Affairs* 73, no. 2 (March-April 1994): 74.

14. Editorial, "Russia's Near Abroad: The West Needs a Policy for
the Russian periphery," *Times*, September 28, 1993.

Index